1432496

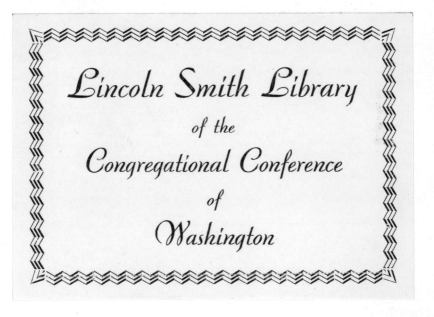

The
Philosophical Heritage
of the Christian Faith

The
Philosophical Heritage
of the Christian Faith

By

HAROLD A. BOSLEY, Ph.D.

1 9 4 4

WILLETT, CLARK & COMPANY

CHICAGO   NEW YORK

To

EDWARD SCRIBNER AMES

*Preacher, Philosopher, Writer
Teacher, Friend*

Preface

THE CONTENTS of this book are a series of lectures given to the Pastors' Institute held at the University of Chicago during the summer of 1943. The lecture form has been retained throughout, in the belief that it would make for somewhat easier reading.

Although prepared for a ministerial group, the lectures deal with themes that should be of equal concern to many laymen. We have fallen on desperate days indeed if only ministers are interested in the intellectual heritage of our faith. For from the beginning laymen have supplied the steady expanding power which has made Christianity one of the distinctive religions of the world. No branch of the Christian church has built up a hereditary priestly class; the leadership has been steadily recruited from the laity. This is one of the reasons why the Christian tradition has kept as close to the earth as it has. Even in those ages which seem to us in retrospect to have been primarily "otherworldly," powerful bonds kept the church aware of this world and of the human problems encountered in this life. This, more than anything else, constitutes the reason for the truth in Professor Hocking's famous statement that "religion is the prolific mother of culture." Such could not have been the case had religion been wholly or even predominantly otherworldly in attitude and purpose. Each generation of leaders is fresh from the homes and normal associations and problems of family and community life. No monastery is isolated enough to separate a man from this background. Consequently the church is kept, willy-nilly, in close, constant and creative contact with ordinary human problems and aspirations.

All of which underlines the importance of reawakening

among ministers and laymen alike an awareness of the existence of a great intellectual tradition in Christianity.   This
consciousness is one of our guarantees against provincialism
in concern and intolerance in thought — two of the greatest
evils in modern civilization.   When we realize the extent of
our indebtedness to both Greek and barbarian, to both Jew
and gentile, a debt extending and accumulating over nearly
twenty centuries, we can never be quite content to think
merely in terms of " me and my wife, my son John and his
wife."   Nor will we feel like chanting with the Red Queen,
" Everyone's heads off but our own."

A special word may be in order to readers who have not
been trained in philosophy or who are not accustomed to
reading philosophical literature, some examples of which
occur in the Appendix.   Here, as in most specialized fields,
the bark of the vocabulary is worse than the bite.   If you will
arm yourself with a comprehensive general dictionary and
the *Dictionary of Philosophy* recently put out by the Alliance
Book Corporation, you will be able to challenge and secure
the meaning of most of the technical words (metaphysics,
idealism, realism, etc.) which are likely to be encountered.
Plato and Aristotle are no harder to read than Calvin, Luther
and Augustine — and it is of unparalleled importance that
leaders in Christian churches should know this from first-hand
experience.   If the great minds of the ages are at home in our
studies, we who preach shall be more effective ministers of
Jesus Christ to this generation.

I trust that the book will not give the impression that the
benefits in the relationship between philosophy and religion
have all gone from philosophy to religion.   This would be
wholly false to the facts.   A highly useful book could be written on the theme, " The Religious Heritage of Philosophy,"
but it would be a different book from this one.   Also, it would
have been possible to extend the area of these lectures to include studies of how philosophical ideas have influenced the
development of specific theological doctrines like God, the

Trinity, Logos, Christ, Immortality, etc. What I have done here is no more than a sketchy introduction to so comprehensive a history of theology.

The appendix of the book is self-explanatory. It constitutes a brief but, I hope, useful introduction to some of the great pieces of philosophical literature and gives suggestions as to how and where to proceed in broadening and deepening one's acquaintance with the masters.

The main part of the appendix consists of excerpts from the writings of Plato, Aristotle and Plotinus, since they, beyond all other classical philosophers, are a decisive influence in the intellectual framework of the Christian faith. This was true in the early centuries of Christian theology and it continues to be true today, though other and perhaps equally decisive influences are now felt in the realm of thought. But there is no disputing the fact that an adequate understanding and appreciation of Christian thought is impossible apart from a careful and comprehensive knowledge of the philosophy of these three masters. Their influence on the Christian tradition was not always direct; frequently, and for nearly thirteen hundred years, only fragments of their writings were known to Christian thinkers. The accidents of history, in addition to the painstaking work of scholars, have given us a fuller knowledge of their writings than either Augustine or Aquinas possessed. But he would be a hardy soul who would proclaim that we therefore understand Aristotle better than Aquinas did!

In the opinion of Dean Inge, one of the most reliable students of Neo-Platonism, Plotinus, the greatest of that school, is the man to watch if contemporary religious thought is to find its way out of such dilemmas as mind versus matter, spirit versus body, ideal versus real, reason versus faith, etc. That is high praise — too high, perhaps — but the fact is that Plotinus is not widely known even among Christians who seek to be intellectually alert. It is hoped that the two excerpts from his writings which appear in the appendix will stimulate the kind of further attention that his work deserves.

The bibliography lists, first, books *about* philosophy and books of selections from the writings of the pivotal thinkers whom we have been mentioning all through the lectures. This leads naturally into the second section, which is an invitation to stand in what I have come reluctantly to regard as the most attractive spot in Dante's entire scheme of things: Limbo or the first circle of Hell! Here we are "in the midst of a philosophic company": Socrates, Plato, Aristotle ("the master of those who know"), Plotinus, Epictetus, and all the others whose reflections have been a light unto our pathway. I cannot help feeling that if Dante had been more of a philosopher he would surely have given them a more congenial abode. In this section we profit exceedingly by the fine publications of the basic works of the ancient philosophers only recently made available at moderate prices by various publishing houses, notably Random House and the University of Chicago Press.

There is no adequate way to express my gratitude to the ministers who constituted and the leaders who conducted the Pastors' Institute at which these lectures were given. One's confidence in the vigorous intellectual condition of the contemporary church is fortified by such associations. I am deeply indebted to many persons: to Dr. Albert Palmer, president of the Chicago Theological Seminary, and to Dr. Henry Nelson Wieman of the University of Chicago for their encouragement to present the lectures in book form; to Miss Helen Hayes of Baltimore for her expert assistance in typing the appendix; to Mrs. T. H. Mattheiss, Jr., my secretary, who has put in many hours over the manuscript, doing so thorough a job with it all the way from the preface to the index that, if she were minded to do so, there is a real sense in which she could call it "my book"; to Miss Grace Turnbull, my neighbor and friend, for permission to quote the lengthy sections from Plotinus in the appendix.

I wish to thank the following publishers for permission to

quote from their books and other publications: Charles Scribner's Sons; Duell, Sloan & Pearce; Harper & Brothers; Henry
Holt & Company; Liveright Publishing Corporation; the Macmillan Company; Prentice-Hall, Inc.; Simon & Schuster. The
quotation from Antonio Aliotta is to be found on page 410 of
his *Idealistic Reaction against Science,* published by the Macmillan Company (1914); that from Frederick W. Robertson,
on page 134 of his *Sermons,* published by Harper & Brothers.

HAROLD A. BOSLEY

Mount Vernon Place Methodist Church
Baltimore, Maryland

Contents

The
Philosophical Heritage
of the Christian Faith

A philosopher is one who is not content merely to live, but who is capable of reflecting upon life; who is not the plaything of time, but can establish his dominion over it by placing himself in the infinite moment of which it forms part. The fullest life of the real, and its most intimate possession — the aspiration of every philosopher — are not to be found in immediate experience, in the intuitive data which are but fragments of reality no less abstract in their seeming concreteness than the concepts of the intellectualist, but rather in concrete thought, which does not efface the moment of life but rather raises it to a higher degree of truth, showing it to us in the light of all its relations to the rest of the universe.

ANTONIO ALIOTTA —
Idealistic Reaction against Science

. I .

Philosophy—The Handmaid
of Religion

MEDIEVAL philosophers gloried in the distinction implied in the metaphor: philosophy — the handmaid of theology. They thought it the summit of praise to have their efforts regarded as performing the menial tasks in the household
of " the Queen of the Sciences." For the most part they bus-
ied themselves happily at the endless work of burnishing dogmas, brushing away the cobwebs of ignorance and, in their
high moments, exposing and disposing of heretics — the ro-
dents or devils of the establishment. But many of these men
proved to be downright headstrong in the performance of
such duties. Alcuin, Roger Bacon, Abelard, Duns Scotus —
to name only a few — were far from being shy servants of
the queen. Their impertinence kept them in constant trouble with her majesty's more orthodox servants. Not that that
fact abashed them! You cannot read Thomas Aquinas without finally regarding him as the sort of servant who dominates
the entire household, including the queen herself.

This medieval conception of the role of philosophy in life
had at least as many advantages as handicaps. Philosophers
had a definite body of vital material to work with; i.e., a view
of life, of the world, of history and of God which was thought
to be the only door to a happy eternal destiny. Hence philosophy had a crucial task to do. She was responsible for the
exposition of this view to the believers lest their faith grow
dim. She was its recognized champion when the pagan and

the heretic issued a challenge to combat. Philosophy did not
have to bargain or beg for a place in the schools of the period; she was certain of a warm welcome and was embraced
by many of the keenest minds of the day.

The handicaps suffered by philosophy in this relationship
have been listed so often that we need only mention them
now. The curb on creative ventures in thought which threatened to overstep the limits of orthodoxy in theology; the
ready and cruel reprisals that the church could, and frequently did, inflict upon courageous thinkers whose quest for
truth led them to dangerous conclusions; the constant confusion of worlds of discourse in which, for example, the piety
of Bernard could refute the logic of Abelard or the appeal to
tradition on the part of some prominent churchmen could
block Roger Bacon's thrust toward an experimentalist point
of view — no one, I take it, is disposed to minimize the damage done by such handicaps. Granted, they are not inherent in the medieval principle of the correct relationship between philosophy and theology; they nonetheless are actually
quite inseparable from any probable practice of the principle.

What medieval philosophers gloried in, many modern philosophers would writhe under. What to one was an award of
merit is to the other a badge of shame. Address a contemporary philosopher as a " servant of theology " and watch him
simmer — if not worse! Modern philosophy — i.e., philosophical movements since the seventeenth century — has regarded
herself as an independent, critical and creative discipline, and
as fully the equal of theology, science and the arts in her contribution to human welfare. She has written histories of her
own development which as a rule convey her dislike for the
medieval epoch. They dwell at great length upon the classical period of Greek and Roman thought; they then hurry over
what is by any reckoning the longest span of philosophy's historical career during which she was under the surveillance of
the Christian churches; they finally slow down and expand
again almost to classical proportions as they discuss what has

happened since the seventeenth century. It is hard to avoid the conclusion that many modern philosophers are ashamed of those fourteen hundred years in which their intellectual forefathers were honored, though hard-worked and closely watched, servants in the household of theology.

While that is primarily a problem for the historians of philosophy to wrestle with, anyone who is interested in the intellectual foundations of the Christian faith finds himself involved in it too. Just as philosophers cannot avoid either confessing or acclaiming the imprint of Christian theology upon their discipline, so Christian theologians cannot honestly deny — nor should they want to — the fact that the mark of philosophy can be found in every doctrine and dogma, in every ideal and code, in every institution and rite which we cherish as fundamental to the Christian tradition. We are witnessing a revival, amounting almost to a reformation, of interest in religion on the part of philosophers. The idea that philosophy and religion could be kept separate in any thoroughgoing sense is now widely acknowledged to be pure mythology. Whenever philosophy toils at the problems of metaphysics, or logic, or esthetics, or ethics, or knowledge, she is putting her shoulder under some of the burdens of religion. Increasingly, though reluctantly, philosophers are recognizing this, and that fact can mean great good for the future of both philosophy and religion if religious leaders recognize it, too, and are willing to understand and accept the assistance which philosophy can render. This is one of the two major reasons why I have chosen the philosophical heritage of the Christian faith as the theme for these discussions.

The second reason is this: In a day of confusion amounting to chaos men invariably seek direction and order by harking back to " fundamentals." Professor A. N. Whitehead somewhere says that incoherence is a state in which a man has lost contact with first principles. It is hard to find a more apt description of our own day. We are seeking to conquer our incoherence by recapturing the first principles upon which we have been trying to build this civilization. Every ideal and institution is re-examining and reappraising its tradition in search of such "fundamentals." This search is going on as industriously within as outside the Christian churches. We shall surely find that our search for the fundamental ideals and ideas of the Christian tradition will lead us straight into an evaluation of an inheritance in which philosophy and religion are fused beyond all separation. The effort of some contemporary theologians and theological movements to by-pass this fact and treat religion as a thing apart makes interesting reading, but it will not persuade anyone who has more than a speaking acquaintance with the development of our religious tradition. Philosophy is moving to reclaim her religious heritage, and we in religion would be well advised to reclaim and re-evaluate our philosophical heritage.

I am convinced that as we do this, not alone in this formal fashion but more especially in the privacy of our individual studies, we shall be making an indispensable kind of preparation for the enormously exacting task of preaching in wartime. How can this sort of investigation be an aid to our main job? you ask. And I reply by calling your attention to the following considerations.

1. A careful study of our intellectual heritage emphasizes the fact that our message has grown to greatness through a long tradition; a tradition in which reason and mystical ecstasy, experiment and convention, change and permanence have left their mark. For all its baffling complexity the Christian tradition comes to a head, so far as our job as preachers is concerned, in this simple purpose: We are called to confront this generation with the fact of God as we see him in Jesus Christ. Which, in translation, means that we are called to preach a historically tested and validated way and view of life to moderns who are scared to death by their grim contact with the brutal realities of history and with the ethical rigors of the universe in which we live. The historical hour in which we live and work is much too grave for the kind of hysterical

utterances which we too frequently hear and which — let us confess it — we are constantly tempted to make. We shall fall far short of our duty as Christian preachers if we fail to confront the hysterics of the hour with the documented realization that the message we preach is rooted and grounded in a set of facts that are as nearly tested and verified as the relativities and contingencies of history permit.

2. A second reason for this sort of study at this particular time is closely related to the one just given. It affirms the fact that religion is relevant to the problems of today because it has grown to maturity in terms of the problems and experiences of other days. It is of utmost importance not to yield to the contemporary insistence that in view of the extra-special character of the crisis in which civilization finds itself we must bring forth some kind of super-duper spiritual magic which will calm our fears and rock the screaming children back into ethical slumberland. Religion — at least a historically rooted Christianity — does not have a series of answers in capsule form which it can quickly dispense to anyone or any age suffering, as God knows we are, from a serious spiritual malady. Paul's word to the Philippians may seem hard, but it is true; we must work out our own salvation in fear and trembling. Paul most assuredly did not mean that faith in Christ does not help a man in his struggle for salvation. That is precisely the point he was making in his letter to the Romans. But he was saying, what we too must say, that the truth which was in Christ cannot be had for the asking. A man must be prepared to wrestle against every conceivable power, whether natural or supernatural, in order to win and keep the Faith. This epitomizes our task today. Whatever truth we confront our people with in the name of our faith, is a hard-won, often tested truth. Every belief, rite, custom and ethical precept has a long biography, extending over many centuries and enriched by the variety of human experiences which have become a part of its essential character. We must never forget that it is possible for us to preach only

because " other men labored and [we] are entered into their labors."

The painstaking work of Harnack in *The Mission and Expansion of Christianity* and of Latourette in *The Expansion of Christianity* — to cite only the two most inclusive studies — sets forth in abundant detail the character of these labors of our spiritual forebears. They are labors of the earth, earthy, to say the least. They are much more than the heroic endurance of martyrs and the faithfulness of believers during the dramatic periods of persecution, important as these were. They are the quarreling of the Corinthian Christians to whom Paul wrote letters devoted to many problems, some harrowing and some humdrum. They are the expositions of the faith by Clement of Alexandria and Origen in the face of and by means of some of the dominant ideals of Platonic philosophy. They include the efforts of individual Christians who spoke to their comrades in toil of Christ's saving power and thus made possible the swift, sure spread of Christianity over the first three centuries. They include the effective charitable endeavors of the early church which made it a powerful force for good in the life of common people. They include the journeys of the tens of thousands of missionaries who left home and people in order that Christ might be preached to the ends of the earth. They include the scholarly undertakings of men like Jerome, Augustine, Melanchthon and the entire host of those who have sought to clarify the faith. They include the simple, firmly held convictions of laymen as well as the great summations of thought of Augustine and Aquinas.

And the end of such labors is not yet in sight. Our labors likewise are being fed into the loom of Christian history, and we hope other generations may profit by them even as we do by what has gone before us.

All of which is an old truth to you — but to remember it is one of our greatest guarantees against the kind of fruit-fly thinking and preaching which today is weakening the Christian witness even though it is loudly applauded by a world

which seeks solace for suffering by some less difficult path
than that of repentance of sins. No one knows better than
a preacher how hard it is to bring an insight born of human
experience to bear steadily upon some unsolved problem in
present events. Yet it is our work to try to throw the light of
tested religious conviction upon the " darkling plain " which
is

> " Swept with confused alarms of struggle and flight,
>   Where ignorant armies clash by night."

This task is doubly difficult if we begin to doubt the usefulness of the light we are trying to throw into the dark re-
cesses of human problems. Let that happen and we are in
the clutch of a real spiritual crisis, one from which we must
literally be rescued by an act of God or man, or, more ac-
curately, by an act of God through man. That many of us
find ourselves in this plight is seen in the speedy fashion in
which schools of disciples have formed around several of the
splendid theological thinkers of our day: Karl Barth, Reinhold Niebuhr and Henry Nelson Wieman, to mention the
three best known to us in America. We who are supposedly
the light-bearers in a day of darkness find ourselves mum-
bling with the mob, " Which is the way where light dwelleth? " Or we find ourselves flinching under the query, " Can
the blind lead the blind? "

What I am contending in this series of talks is this: The
only way out of the predicament of having lost confidence
either in ourselves or in the worth of what we do as Christian
preachers, or in both, is the hard way of reappraising the
world view of the Christian faith. We shall not find that
world view lacking — of that I am firmly convinced. But it
will never be able to secure its proper expression in and
through us until and unless we come to terms with it by way
of understanding and personal commitment. While philosophy knows no " Open sesame " to the closed doors of many
spiritual crises, it can render invaluable assistance to anyone

who seeks to "prove all things," "to give a reason for the hope that is within us." In fact, it has proved its worth steadily throughout the whole historical career of the Christian faith. This contribution has been so conspicuous in what Canon Charles Raven refers to as the "best periods" of theology [1] — i.e., in the third century with Origen, in the thirteenth with Aquinas, and in the seventeenth with the Cambridge Platonists — that the onus of proof rests upon anyone who doubts its ability to render material assistance again today. A short time spent with any one of these pivotal periods will make clear the kind of assistance that philosophy can render in an age of intellectual confusion.

The first of these "best" periods covers a much longer span than the life and work of Origen, though he is one of the most important figures in it. Actually it begins with the Christian invasion of the centers of Greek culture and culminates in the Augustinian synthesis. The second period begins with the development and spread of orthodoxy in the Christian church and culminates in the *Summa* of Thomas Aquinas. The third period lies in the seventeenth century, when an emerging empirical science was beginning to challenge the medieval synthesis, and culminates in the efforts of religious spirits to place their faith on the foundation of Platonic idealism. While it would be possible to study these creative epochs in many ways, I want to center attention for the moment upon the interplay between philosophy and religion. Notice I said "interplay," because in each of these eras philosophy was learner as well as teacher. Although philosophy and religion frequently said harsh things about each other, we who study these periods from afar cannot avoid the conclusion that they lifted each other to a new level of relevance and usefulness in human life.

In the first period we see a Jewish sect taking root in a world actuated by a quite different view of life and destiny. Christianity moved from a world in which the average man believed in *God* to one in which he believed in *gods;* from a

world in which the awareness of God's will as a personal
was studiously cultivated to one in which men could choose
between charging events up to the caprice of gods or to an
impersonal world order, the result in either case being a sense
of fatalism and irresponsibility. Long before Christianity
came on the scene the philosophical tradition in Greece had
challenged the anthropomorphic and multitudinous deities
of the pantheon. Practically every philosopher of note had
subjected them to criticism which at times degenerated into
ridicule. But most of these philosophers had little better food
to offer, or so it seemed to the average man, who appears to
have gone right on making his peace with the divinities of the
pantheon or with the new and mysterious deities of the salvation cults that flourished throughout Greece from the fifth
century B.C. on. Woe betide the dramatist who caused one of
his agents to speak disrespectfully of any of the folk deities!
Several tried it but wound up begging mercy from an aroused
populace. One of the most fascinating chapters in the history of philosophy is concerned with the way in which the
Platonic tradition (including for the moment the work and
influence of Socrates and Aristotle) challenged both the divinities of the pantheon and the idea of an impersonal world
order. Unfortunately for an adequate acknowledgment of
this early debt to Platonism, we cannot go into the details of
the conflict whereby the pivotal thinkers of Greece struggled
against those reactionary elements in Greek thought which
persisted until Christianity won a final victory nearly four
centuries later. But in winning her victory Christianity used
every weapon in the armory of Platonism and Neo-Platonism,
as well as the weapons which were uniquely her own, such as
scriptural authority, the doctrine of the messiah, and certain
other clearly defined ideas of Jewish theology and the primitive church.

If time permitted, it would be well worth our while to
study in detail the way in which the religious faith of Palestinian Christianity grew to the stature of the Augustinian syn-

thesis; but even within the limits which we must observe we can sketch the historical drama that unfolded in many different places in the ancient world. We get a clear picture of it in the lives of two Christian teachers in Alexandria, Clement (150–215) and Origen (175–254). Alexandria was the center of a flourishing renascence of Greek culture at that time. It was famous for its libraries and schools and for the range of freedom it usually allowed new doctrine. To be sure the Christian groups in that city suffered occasionally from mob violence, but generally they and their schools functioned unmolested.

Clement had been brought up in a Hellenism which was the truest descendant of classical Greek culture that could be found. He had a respect for Plato that amounted to reverence and was deeply impressed by the moral principles of Stoicism. All of this, let us remember, before he became a convert to Christianity. How, when and why he took this step we are not sure, but it seems to have been connected with his study under Pantaenus, then the head of the Christian school in Alexandria. Until Pantaenus' death Clement served under him in the school, succeeding him as teacher when he died. So far from abandoning his Hellenism when he became a Christian, Clement worked the two together. As Dr. Case observes, " he believed that philosophy had been given to the Greeks, as the Law had been given to the Jews, to prepare them to receive Christ. Clement had absorbed substantial elements of both Platonism and Stoicism, and used them extensively in his interpretation of Christianity." [2] He taught a profound respect for the rational faculty as a divinely ordained gift of man. He believed that true knowledge, always rooted in love, enables a Christian to rise higher in the scale of virtue than would otherwise be possible. That Clement owes these emphases to Platonism no student of the *Republic* will doubt for one moment. Combined with them are certain other teachings that are as distinctly Jewish: that the Scriptures are God's revealed word, and that through the

Jewish people God had prepared the way for Christ's rule on earth. Clement welded these various views together into an apologetic that played havoc with current polytheism and challenged the Gnostic schools which were then flourishing in Alexandria. He was an ardent churchman, believing in the sacraments, the apostolic tradition and the saving power of prayer. He seems to have accepted the simple Christology which affirmed the uniqueness of Christ as the Son of God. The tangled questions implicit in this formula were yet to be raised and explored by his pupil, Origen, by Arius, Athanasius and others.

It may not be necessary to stress the fact that Clement was no indiscriminate borrower from the philosophy of earlier Greece. As Dr. McGiffert points out, he denounced the "materialism of Democritus and the hedonism of Epicurus . . . in unmeasured terms," and "he likened the Sophists to old shoes which are all worn out except the tongue." [3] But always when the going got hard on some problem of knowledge and understanding, Clement's answers were connected with roots that ran back to Plato's school.

What happened to Clement happened to many other important leaders in early Christian history. Men deeply versed in the point of view of the prevailing culture, whether the Hellenism of the eastern Mediterranean regions or the Latinism of the west, stepped into the Christian fold both as learners and as teachers. It is not too much to say that they brought with them the intellectual framework of what was later to become the orthodoxy of the Christian church. In their ideas and influence, as in their persons, we find the outlines of the synthesis that was to bring Christian faith and Greek philosophy into an inescapable union.

This was especially true of Origen, and at a later date of Augustine, whose stories are more or less common knowledge in the Christian tradition. All I desire to stress here is the incalculable importance of Neo-Platonism to both of them. While, on the surface of their writings, it does not have anything like the influence of scriptural authority, as a matter of logical fact it is used steadily by both of them to provide a world view in terms of which scriptural authority might reasonably be accepted. Origen laid the basis for much if not most of the theologizing which was done throughout the third and fourth centuries. His catholic mind raised every major problem that, in the course of later disputes, was the subject of such bitter contention that anathemas were common and mob violence not infrequent. When Western or Latin Christianity triumphed over Eastern or Greek Christianity the name of Origen went into eclipse, but his ideas on the being of God, on the relationship between the Father and the Son, and on the relationship between the temporal and the eternal spheres of reality continued to influence Christian thought.

Augustine was driven into Neo-Platonism by the inadequacy of another type of philosophy known as Manichaeism. Perplexed in his thought and hounded in his person by the fact of evil, he simply could not rest until he had some sort of explanation of its relationship to a good God, in whose reality he believed long before he became a Christian. Neo-Platonism furnished the answer that satisfied him. "He found in Neo-Platonism much to attract him," Dr. McGiffert writes; "the conception of a realm of spiritual being altogether different from the realm of things, the notion that all visible objects are but the types or expressions of invisible ones, the belief in the immateriality and immortality of the soul and in man's possession of a spiritual sense by which he may know God and the realities of the unseen world. Most of all he was influenced by the Neo-Platonic solution of the problem of evil. . . . According to Plotinus, evil is in itself nothing, it is simply the absence of good. . . . It came like a new gospel and encouraged him to think that truth might not be wholly inaccessible after all and to resume feverishly the search which he had abandoned in despair." [4] "It was no great step from Platonism to Christianity as he understood them," Dr. McGiffert concludes.[5]   Then for a period of thirty-five years Augustine worked so vigorously at the task of bringing an over-all pattern of order into Christian theology, and achieved such signal success, that his authority was dominant in the Catholic Church for nearly a thousand years.   He may rightly be regarded as the father of orthodoxy for that period, and for our purpose we need only note the fact that the skeletal framework of his thought was thoroughly Greek in character.

It is a familiar story how Aquinas found the mind of the church sadly addled by the various heresies that had sprung up, as well as by brilliant questioners and critics of orthodoxy like Abelard.   But the greatest threat of all lay in the newly discovered works of Aristotle, whose thought had served Moslem theologians much as Plato's had served Christians. The logical rigor of Aristotle simply would not square with the inconsistencies which the mystical and more or less impulsive Augustine had written into the character of orthodoxy.   This was so apparent that certain churchmen were all for declaring Aristotle a heretic — and in truth they had to do either that or else groom him for sainthood!   This latter task fell to Aquinas, and he performed it to perfection.   His *Summa* is the official philosophy and theology of the Catholic Church today.   It is also the center of renewed study and interest on the part of many thinkers who, while not of Roman Catholic persuasion, are nonetheless interested in the intellectual orderliness which so clearly reigns in his thought.

Let me guard against a possible misunderstanding which may grow out of my repeated reference to the influence of Greek philosophers.   I do not mean to give the impression that they are the only creative thinkers to emerge in the Western world, though so eminent an authority as Whitehead somewhere remarks that the whole of philosophy since Plato has consisted of dropping footnotes to one of his dialogues, the *Timaeus*.   Be that as it may, the point I desire to make is this: In an age of intellectual confusion in religion, theology always falls back on some world view, some philosophy, which seems to be adequate.

As another instance of this process, the Cambridge Platonists in the seventeenth century were confronted by the materialism, if not the actual atheism, of Hobbes and by a whole train of materialistic influences growing out of the emergence of science. Their answer to this challenge of materialism was couched in terms of Plato's emphasis upon the Eternal Idea in contrast to transient matter.

Modern philosophers have had similar treatment at the hands of theologians, for whether they like it or not we continue to use them in our day of desperation. Descartes, Spinoza, Locke, Kant, Hegel, Lotze, James, Bergson, Kierkegaard, Bowne, Dewey, Whitehead — how large such men loom in any adequate history of modern theology. The problem of how much they owe their philosophic ancestors may be left to them; so far as we are concerned the plain fact is that they have provided the various schools of theology with their intellectual framework, much as Neo-Platonism served Augustine. And with good cause we have turned to them, for they sought to see life steadily and see it whole. You cannot work your way through the writings of any of them without sensing the complete seriousness with which a great mind is weighing facts, appraising logic and making judgments. These men are not unacquainted with mystical vision, with flashes of insight that are prophetic in character, but they are not easy about such deliverances until they have subjected them to every known test of reason and relevance. Roughly speaking, the great goals of philosophic endeavor have been and are knowledge of truth, beauty, and goodness. In order to reach them, philosophy has learned what science, art, and religion have to teach about the fundamental character of the world. She has approached the data supplied by these other disciplines with the venerable query: "How can these things be?" And it is in her various answers to this question that she has made her own distinctive contribution to religion and our common life.

In later lectures we shall consider certain philosophic contributions that have been made to the Christian tradition. In a very real sense our search for God is philosophy's search for reality — a fact which is not so much admitted as affirmed by the leading philosophers. Our search for truth and knowledge is akin to hers; even those of us who think that, in revelation, religion has a special form of knowledge cannot afford to ignore what philosophy has to say about the meaning of truth. Our endeavor properly to appreciate the majesty and mystery of God is one with the sense of wonder in which philosophy begins and ends her quest. Our emphasis upon the full, the abundant life is blood-brother, at least in principle, to her emphasis upon the good life.

But philosophy has gone about her business in her own way. Generally speaking, she has never used a simple word if a difficult one was handy. She has steadily refused to popularize her deepest insights, not because she is unwilling but because she cannot find the words to do it properly. In our investigations we shall be forced to confront with stout heart the hazards of the cumbersome but usually exact terminology which she uses. Yet I am persuaded, and hope to persuade those of you who may need persuasion on the point, that the effort, however hard, will be immensely worth while. Lest you think I am outlining a bugaboo, consider the various general fields or categories of philosophic endeavor. They represent definite areas of specialization in contemporary philosophy, though every philosopher usually moves with freedom in all of them. To sketch them now, even in outline form, will give us some notion of the wide area of human experience which is swept by the nets of philosophy.

1. *Ontology* or *metaphysics* is the study of reality, being and causation. It is the attempt to construct a world view, to depict the essential nature of the universe in which we

live. Metaphysics has usually been the scene of the great philosophic conflicts; which is to be expected, since in it the philosopher attempts to interpret the whole of reality in terms of one or two basic principles. Critics of any given metaphysics usually proceed by way of pointing out the inadequacy of said principles to certain areas of known fact.

2. *Epistemology* is the investigation of the origin, structure, methods and validity of knowledge. It is on the borderline between philosophy and psychology, since the latter is interested in the knowing process. Though the word " epistemology " is a newcomer in the philosophic vocabulary, the problems now covered by it are as old as philosophic endeavor. The problem of valid knowledge is one of the most aggravating that the human mind has encountered. You should be thankful, as I am, that we shall not need to dip very deeply into the many solutions which have been suggested. But it is as plain as the proverbial pikestaff that religion must be profoundly concerned with what such answers add up to.

3. *Logic* is the study of the principles governing valid reasoning. It is closely related to epistemology; too closely, some logicians think! Some of the most venerated thinkers in our cultural tradition have centered their attention in this area. Aristotle is regarded as the father of deductive logic, while the development of inductive logic is regarded as a relatively recent affair. Another recent development is symbolic or formal logic, which in its passion for conveying exact meanings has developed its own special vocabulary, one that looks strangely like an algebraic equation. I suppose we in religion have less patience with the logician than with almost any other philosophic specialist. He is so like the tortoise, inching along from one little fact to another, peering behind every word and inflection in search of hobgoblins. But again he is an excellent antidote for those grandiose conclusions of ours made in a moment of what we think is divine afflatus. The moral to be appended to every book on logic could be drawn up in these words: Humility becometh man. That

this moral is freighted with religious implications none of us will care to deny.

4. We must forgive the philosophers the word *axiology*, but it sounds more vicious than it is. It is the study of the nature, criteria and metaphysical status of value. Like " epistemology," the word itself is a latecomer, but the problems it denotes exercised Plato and his intellectual descendants from that day to this. One branch of axiological endeavor is primarily concerned with the study of moral values and is known as *ethics*. Another branch is concerned with the beautiful and bears the more familiar name of *esthetics*. Religion, especially the Jewish-Christian tradition, has accented ethics more heavily than esthetics through most of its history, but a corrective process seems to be under way today. The field of value-theory is the place where there is a most obvious overlapping of religious and philosophic endeavors. Some first-class rows have already occurred between them, and others seem to be in the offing. When a value-theorist says that values like truth, beauty and goodness are " merely " (sometimes I think the trouble begins in the way he inflects that word!) subjective reactions, thoughtful religionists grab the trumpet and send forth no uncertain call to battle. Conversely, when religionists affirm that these values are wholly outside our experience, the value-theorist usually gives them a severe going-over. Lest I leave the wrong impression by these aggressive similes, let me conclude by saying that good relations are developing as rapidly as can be expected.

So much for the general outline of the fields in which philosophy sows and reaps. Yet the actual human meaning of philosophy is close to the earth of daily life and interests. It might help us to see the tasks of philosophy as they appear to some of the keenest thinkers of our day. Persons who charge philosophy with being too rational, too much occupied with reason, need to study at some length the opinion of Professor A. N. Whitehead, one of the greatest minds of all time: " Reason can be compared to the force of gravitation, the weakest of all natural forces, but in the end the creator of suns and stellar systems — those great societies of the Universe." [6]   Persons who say that philosophy is too abstract, too academic, and who cite chapter and verse from many books in philosophy to prove their point will find an adequate corrective in this statement by Professor M. C. Otto: "The *spirit* of philosophy is the quest for depth and richness of meaning, for wisdom of life, a quest that is endless; abstract formulas, closed systems, pronouncements on ultimates, these are the *letter* of philosophy." [7]   Then there are those who think that philosophy is too far removed from the problems and concerns of the average man. Not only will Professor Otto's statement help them toward a truer picture, but in addition they need to be reminded of Professor Whitehead's statement of "the central problem of metaphysics." You may recall the description of metaphysics that was given a moment ago — the study of reality. Professor Whitehead humanizes that formula to read, "Abide with me, fast falls the eventide." [8]

I submit, in conclusion, that we have much to learn from philosophy, not alone because she has been a firm buttress in periods of distress before, but more especially because she works at many of the problems that are fundamental to religion. She may not again want to be regarded as "the handmaid of religion," and I am in favor of dropping the term if it means that her work is of subordinate importance. Our relationship is a cooperative one and should be carried on in the spirit of cooperation.

REFERENCES

1 Charles Raven, *Science, Religion and the Future* (New York: The Macmillan Co., 1943), p. 10.

2 S. J. Case, *Makers of Christianity* (New York: Henry Holt & Co., 1934), p. 100.

3 A. C. McGiffert, *History of Christian Thought*, 2 vols. (New York: Charles Scribner's Sons, 1932), I, 184–85.

4 *Ibid.*, II, 76–77.

5 *Ibid.*, II, 78.

6 A. N. Whitehead, *Symbolism* (New York: The Macmillan Co., 1927), p. 82.

7 M. C. Otto, *The Human Enterprise* (New York: F. S. Crofts & Co., 1940), p. vii.

8 Quoted by J. S. Bixler, *Religion for Free Minds* (New York: Harper & Brothers, 1939), p. 148.

Truth hath a quiet breast.
Shakespeare — *King Richard II*

And ye shall know the truth and the truth shall make you free.

John 8:32

As for the truth, it endureth, and is always strong; it liveth and conquereth for evermore. With her there is no accepting of persons or rewards; but she doeth the things that are just, and refraineth from all unjust and wicked things; and all men do well like of her works. Neither in her judgment is any unrighteousness; and she is the strength, kingdom, power and majesty of all ages. Blessed be the God of truth.

I Esdras 4:38-4

"I cannot refute you, Socrates," said Agathon. "And let us suppose that what you say is true."
"Say rather, dear Agathon, that you cannot refute the truth; for Socrates is easily refuted."

Plato — *Symposium*

. II .

The Dependability of Truth

PAUL is too frequently quoted in disparagement of philosophy. To be sure he does, in I Corinthians, speak of lovers of wisdom in a less than complimentary way. But he also laid out, perhaps all unknowingly, the outline of the intellectual foundations of Christianity in his famous admonition to the Philippians: "Finally, brethren, whatsoever things are true, whatsoever things are honest, whatsoever things are just, whatsoever things are pure, whatsoever things are lovely, whatsoever things are of good report; if there be any virtue and if there be any praise, think on these things."[1] That advice is all the text we need for proceeding in a forthright way with our examination of the philosophical heritage of the Christian faith.

You will recall that yesterday we spent our time getting a sort of over-all view of the general relations between philosophy and religion. We found them to be deeply interdependent, indeed quite inseparable, so far as the last two thousand years of history in the Western world are concerned. By paying some attention to the life and work of men like Clement of Alexandria, Origen, Augustine, Aquinas and the Cambridge Platonists of the seventeenth century we saw in a hurried way how religion in a day of crisis always falls back on some world view or other which gives promise of being able to order the confusion. Classical Christian theology has made constant use of the intellectual labors of Plato and Aristotle; in fact, we must regard them as two of the most potent influences in the shaping of our theology. We saw too how

21

the great thinkers in every age have exercised a profound influence upon the thought-patterns of the religion of their time. Men like Descartes, Spinoza, Locke, Kant, Hegel, Lotze, Bowne and Whitehead have provided theologians with creative insights and new enthusiasm for rethinking the intellectual framework of religion. Not only did such men establish schools of philosophy; they also, though usually by indirection, established schools of theology. In truth, it could not be otherwise. They were seeking to see life steadily and to see it whole; they were seeking an understanding of truth, beauty and goodness, all of which are precious in the sight of religion; they were seeking grounds for confidence in the human enterprise, in the worth of human thought and effort. These being their concerns, what could be more natural than that leaders in religion should turn to them even as leaders in education and, in some cases, government did? Whether we think religious leaders *should* have turned to them is quite beside the point I am making. That point is the simple historical fact that religious leaders always have done so and in all probability will continue to do so. At least whoever thinks differently must assume the burden of proof.

I am prepared to defend the thesis that Christianity must always make use of whatever tools of wisdom she can lay her hands on, pre-eminently those fashioned by philosophy. Not only is this good for religion, but it is actually an inevitability. Philosophy may not be able to furnish us with all we know on earth and all we need to know, but let us not forget that by and large she has always helped us in our day of desperation. The reason for this confidence in philosophy as the handmaid of religion will become clearer as this and subsequent lectures proceed.

Our subject today is " The Dependability of Truth." That particular phrasing comes from Paul's stouthearted assertion, " God can be depended on." [2] It is reinforced by Arthur Hugh Clough's lines:

"It fortifies my soul to know
That, though I perish, Truth is so:
That, howsoe'er I stray and range,
Whate'er I do, Thou dost not change.
I steadier step when I recall
That, if I slip, Thou dost not fall." [3]

There is, I believe, ample philosophic warrant for this faith of the prophet and the poet in the essential dependability of the world in which we live. In order to appraise this belief let us proceed in this manner: (1) Let us begin by clearing philosophy of the prevalent charge of skepticism and agnosticism or indeed outright atheism. (2) Let us continue by outlining the main points and questions in philosophy's search for truth. (3) We shall then be prepared to ask what it is religion can and should learn from philosophy in regard to truth.

It ought not to take long to clear up the relationship between philosophy and skepticism. There is no better place to begin than by acknowledging the fact that doubt and skepticism have been very active, creative factors in the development of our religious tradition. I, for one, am glad that Amos was profoundly skeptical about the ultimate value of liturgy and ceremonial as an adequate human response to God. I am glad that Jesus was skeptical about the sort of righteousness which can be gained by fulfilling the detailed requirements of ceremonial law. I am glad that Paul was skeptical about the arguments of the Judaizers who wanted all men to come to Christ via the law of ceremonial purity in Judaism. In short, I am glad for the skeptical edge, the ground-clearing aspect, of the thought of every pivotal Christian figure. We ought never to forget that the men we honor most are precisely the ones who were courageous enough to say "no" to some and "yes" to other parts of their religious heritage.

What happened in religion happened in philosophy. Professor T. V. Smith, of the University of Chicago, some years ago wrote a book entitled *Creative Skeptics,* which lists some of the great names in philosophy. In fact, the list of creative skeptics which Professor Smith gives is capable of expansion until it includes some phase of the thought of every creative thinker. Like religious reformers, the creative thinkers got under way as great doubters and skeptics. Socrates got men mad enough to kill him by his habit of being skeptical about their beliefs and motives. Plato's dialogues are one long examination of inadequate theories of the meaning of justice or knowledge or being. I suppose in many ways the accolade of being the most creative skeptic in our long philosophic tradition must go to Aristotle. He amassed, studied and criticized the voluminous philosophical literature of ancient Greece, and when the process of rejection, acceptance and modification was over, a great measure of the richness of his thought had come into existence. Descartes is reputed to have inaugurated the era of modern philosophy by his resolution to doubt everything that could be doubted. He ultimately reached the exceedingly fine point of being unable to doubt the fact that he was doing the doubting. That indubitable fact he accepted as *real,* and using it as the clue to reality he proceeded to build up, in consistency with it, other and ampler ideas, such as the idea of a Perfect Being. Finally after a good deal of earnest intellectual sweating he found himself surrounded with a fairly adequate world — the one in which, to common sense, he had been all the time! But it is interesting to note that he trusted his reason only when he could chart its course along mathematical lines, because to him geometry alone yielded the kind of certainty which is beyond all doubt. His example inspired Spinoza both in doubting and in seeking certainty by way of mathematical form.

I am sure that those of you who are familiar with David Hume have been waiting for his name to be placed on the roll of honor as a creative skeptic. I am of the private opinion that he deserves some sort of special recognition for his extraordinary services as a revealer of religious sham, inadequacy and just plain ignorance. His criticism of naïve supernaturalism and superstition continues to be sobering. He pointed out the weakness of reliance upon miracles as a form of evidence so effectively that no one has had to repeat the performance in the past two hundred years. Small wonder the clergy hated him with a holy hatred. There is some little comfort in the fact that he was not much more popular among his fellow philosophers! His analysis of cause, which was the key word among the philosophers of that period who were seeking to grasp the meaning of the new science, was every bit as devastating for them as his attention to miracle had been to the clergy. Immanuel Kant testified that Hume "shook me out of my dogmatic slumbers." And after a brief period of name-calling and self-pity the theologians buckled down to the task of finding some reliable evidences for the validity of the Christian faith. It is not too much to say that we owe William Paley's celebrated *Evidences of Christianity* to the explosions which Hume's skepticism set off.

It is no accident that philosophy has the reputation among religious folk of being an essentially skeptical discipline. Yet I venture to suggest that, despite all I have been saying "in praise of doubt," this skepticism is more apparent than real. To draw the hackneyed distinction between character and reputation, according to which character is what you are and reputation is what folks think you are, however great reputation philosophy may have as a skeptic her character is actually quite different. *Philosophy is a critical, speculative, rational discipline.* Her purpose is to understand, to learn, to know, and to be able to couch her findings in such fashion that they can be shared with other thinking beings. The materials with which she must work are the inherited interpretations of experience, which invariably are a strange accumulation of valid insight, wishful thinking, and biases born of passion, desire and prejudices. Philosophy's method is that of determining certain criteria for truth, for appraising the worth of this heritage. The result of her efforts is the rejection of some interpretations, the drastic modification of others, and the affirmation of the remainder. When a scientist proceeds to evaluate his scientific inheritance in similar fashion he is praised for his objectivity. We gladly admit that in no other way can he weed out false and inadequate conceptions.

It is therefore obviously a severely limited judgment to say that philosophy and skepticism are synonymous terms. The truer way to put the matter is, I believe, this: *Philosophy has had to develop ways of keeping faith with the fact of our ignorance.* She must keep a strict eye on what we know and do not know. She must be severely critical of all our pretensions to knowledge until she has tested their validity. This, I submit, must be regarded as a thankless task at all times no matter how essential it is. Our ideas, our interpretations of the meaning of experience necessarily run beyond known facts. Once they get beyond the reach of the obvious checkup of immediate experience they not infrequently go hog-wild, as my father used to say when describing some form of incomprehensible and wholly unaccountable behavior on the part of my brothers and sisters. It is philosophy's business to check such proceedings by pointing out wherein the interpretations which must necessarily run beyond experience have actually begun to fly in the face of experience and known fact, and must therefore be regarded as false and dangerous. While we may enjoy seeing this happen to someone else we are constitutionally unfitted to appreciate it when it happens to us.

By and large philosophers are not only acutely aware of the fact that their vocation is not a particularly popular one; they are sincerely humbled by the realization that it is an amazingly precarious one. Philosophy can so easily become a venture in towering human pride and arrogance, a condition in which the limited experience of one person is set up in calm judgment of the worth of the inherited and cumulative experience of many men. One occasionally meets philosophers who have feasted heavily on the bread of intellectual conceit, but they are the exception rather than the rule, and seldom are they the truly creative figures of thought. The average philosopher is as humble and conscientious in the performance of his work as is the theologian or the scientist. Humility, along with sincerity and clarity, is an essential virtue in philosophic method.

Let us, to sum up this line of thought, leave the matter at this point: Philosophy is essentially a critical, speculative discipline. Its purpose is understanding and appreciation rather than pontifical pronouncement. In its critical moods it raises questions as to meaning, evidence, and the relationship of interpretation to fact. In its speculative moods it makes imaginative excursions into or constructions of an order of reality or being, clues to which it believes it has found in certain kinds of experience.

The nonskeptical character of philosophy is clearly seen in the careful way in which it has developed the theory of probable truth or, as it is more popularly known, the theory of probability. An imposing literature on this problem has been accumulating over the past two hundred years. Needless to say, a good many theories of probability have been advanced, and they are quite diverse in character. But they are agreed in this very important affirmation: *knowledge is possible.* They may and do disagree upon why and to what degree it is possible, but they can be brought into a common front against any notion that knowledge is a snare and a delusion. The reality of the universe as mediated in and through human experience, for all the baffling and obscure problems encountered therein, is essentially dependable. This conclusion alone is sufficient to clear philosophy of the charge of being skeptical in character. I repeat, philosophy has developed a truly elaborate equipment for being faithful to the fact of our ignorance; and for this she deserves our gratitude.

The philosophical quest for truth involves the asking and

answering of three questions: (1) Where do you look for truth? (2) How do you look for it? (3) What do you find?

Any careful consideration of such questions must begin by noting that the concept "truth" is generally used in two related but quite different ways. In one sense, truth is a judgment as to the value of a proposition. It is the assertion of knowledge. When we observe the rain and say, "It is raining," we have made a statement which is true; i.e., it has a reliable and verifiable knowledge-content. In the second sense, "truth" is a synonym for "reality," for the essential character, or stuff, as the philosophers like to say, of the universe. When Pilate put the question "What is truth?," we may safely assume, he was making a cynical inquiry as to whether there is any objectively real order of reality in terms of which his contemplated action might be wrong and the accused person standing before him might be right. These two meanings of "truth" are different in that one has to do with our knowledge of reality and the other with the character of reality itself. Archbishop Temple suggests that some confusion could be avoided if we would get into the habit of using the word "knowledge" instead of "truth" when we talk about what we know of reality and reserving "truth" for the character or nature of reality. But it is hard to alter so ingrained a philosophic habit as this dual usage of "truth." So far as our present purpose is concerned, the two meanings are closely related in that both have to do with dependability of reality as known; so the two uses of the concept are not wholly contradictory.

It is not as easy to answer that first question, Where do you look for truth? as might appear on the surface. When we answer, "In experience," we seem not to have said as much as we might think. While it is patently true that if truth is to mean anything at all it must come in experience, a not so merry war has been fought among philosophers from Plato right on down as to what phases or aspects of experience are to be regarded as mediating truth. For Plato, truth as reality is to be found in the realm of Eternal Ideas; and truth as knowledge is to be found in those fleeting memories of having glimpsed this realm somewhere, somehow, perhaps in a previous existence, perhaps as a result of an analysis which finally finds itself baffled by a fact which is both real and yet too elusive to be grasped. The famous Socratic dialectic was merely a most effective way of decreasing the number of places in which the desired truth might be hiding, but Socrates never pretended that he was able to reduce these places to one and thus finally lay his hands on the struggling fact of truth itself. He and his great pupils after him were masters at this general procedure. Plato and Aristotle went farther than Socrates in their affirmations of the character of reality, Plato calling it the abode of Eternal Ideas, Aristotle calling it the realm or category of pure Form. They agreed in this, that whoever sought the truth would find it not in individual items of existence (though he would necessarily begin with them) but in the class or form to which this instance or item belonged. The truth or reality of man, for example, is not to be found in individual men; it must be sought in that common human nature by virtue of which we are all men, of which we are instances.

If you ask what all this has to do with the Christian faith, I would reply that, historically at any rate, it was the nub of one of the bitterest yet most creative controversies waged in the Middle Ages — the controversy between realism and nominalism. Realism contended that truth resided in the universal rather than in the particular. Nominalism affirmed the opposite, taking as its position the argument suggested by an early Greek thinker who criticized Plato's Ideas in this fashion: " Horses I see, but ' horseness ' I do not see." The church was vitally involved in the controversy. The future of orthodoxy was at stake. If the realists were right, doctrine and dogma, dealing as they did with universals, could be sustained. If the nominalists were right, all such general pronouncements were not worth the paper they were written on.

Aquinas is regarded by so careful a thinker as Jacques Maritain [4] as having been raised up of God to deliver the church from her indecision. This he did by insisting upon a " both-and " formula rather than the " either-or " one. There is but one truth, he argued, but religion and philosophy discover it in different though related ways. The unique road to truth which religion presents is that of faithful acceptance of the truth as revealed in the doctrine and dogma of the church; i.e., revealed truth. The unique road to truth opened by philosophy is that of intellectual discernment of the essential unities among the particular items of experience — which is rational truth. So far from being outmoded, Thomas' answer (with necessary adaptations, of course) keeps bobbing up in one form or another in Catholic, Protestant and Jewish thought even today.

I wish I could report that philosophers have finally agreed upon an answer to the question, Where do you look for truth? But as I indicated a moment ago the argument still goes on and there seems to be little hope of stopping it. That fact however need not be depressing because there is pretty general agreement that we do find whatever truth we have somewhere in the area of experience. The absolute minimum in describing the matter is reached with the statement that philosophers find something in experience which is at least dependable enough to argue about and with.

The second question, How do you look for truth? has already been partially considered in the course of considering the first one. The historic answers of philosophy are: (1) You look for it by reason. (2) You look for it by intuition. To these, classical Christian thought has added a third way, revelation. On the surface it would seem that all philosophers would agree that reason is the road to truth, but such is not the case. All will agree that reason should be used as long as it helps, but some of the greatest minds have doubted whether it took us anything like as far as intuition. One cannot read Plato without being struck by the fact that he almost

invariably clinches his argument by means of a myth, an alle-
gory, like that of the charioteer in the *Phaedrus* or of the men
in the cave in the *Republic*. Actually this amounts to saying,
" We've reached the limit of our ability to use concepts in a
meaningful way, but there is more, much more truth crying
for expression." In our own day three philosophic leaders,
Henri Bergson, George Santayana and Nicolai Hartmann,
make extended use of intuition as the way in which we grasp
essential truth. The fact that they have fashioned radically
different philosophies might, at first glance, seem to be a re-
pudiation of the validity of intuition (since they ought to in-
tuit the same thing!), but it is equally probable that each is
reporting with complete fidelity his experience of a reality
which is too large, too deep, too mysterious to be grasped in
its entirety by even the steadiest intuitional experience of any
given individual, however gifted. It is at this point that the
philosopher tends to become a poet, since intuition is the
poet's pathway to truth.

I do not think it is possible to give an adequate description of what is meant by intuition. By this I do not mean to
say that intuition is an uncommon experience. Quite to the
contrary, it seems to be much more common than is usually
supposed, but it is the kind of experience that we can describe
only in the most labored way. I am tempted to say of it what
some philosopher said to his class as they approached the
concepts " time " and " space ": " If you know what I mean by
these concepts, let's talk about them. If you don't, let's talk
about something else." But so far as understanding intuition
is concerned the situation is not quite that hopeless. We experience intuition when we " get the point," as we say, of
someone else's argument, or the instructor's lecture, or the
artist's work. Such a statement means that what have been
separated items of experience are suddenly, unaccountably,
fused into a unity of meaning. Two years ago I read a statement, attributed to Nietzsche, to the effect that even if we
were to lose the gospel records we could re-create them from

Bach's oratorio, *The Passion according to St. Matthew*. "Now there," I thought, "is a philosopher who is badly off the beam." But I had not heard the oratorio when I thought that. We got the recording of it some time later, and I settled down to listen in a somewhat skeptical frame of mind. The doubting mood lasted until that loveliest of all arias — the one beginning, "O sacred head now wounded" — was sung; at which point, and quite unaccountably, I found myself in the attitude of having complete faith in the goodness of a God who so loved the world that he gave his only begotten Son. Then I realized that I understood what Nietzsche was talking about. But did I really understand him? my skeptical demon wants to know. Was my subjective reaction to the oratorio exactly like his? Who knows or would be so bold as to hazard a guess? All I am saying is that I was finally at peace with a judgment that had previously perplexed me.

Such intuitional experiences are quite common among us all. Therefore reliance upon intuition by the artist and thinker is a much more down-to-earth procedure than we sometimes think it is and, I must say, than some of them occasionally pretend it is. To say this in no wise strips intuition of its meaning; it simply removes the mask of novelty, if not magic, which is all too commonly placed upon it. When philosophy relies on intuition, then, it is not necessarily either defying reason or flying in the face of facts. It may be simply reaching beyond reason and discovering a new and deeper relationship among facts.

So far as revelation is concerned it cannot, strictly speaking, be considered *a philosophic answer* to the question, How shall we look for truth? As I indicated earlier, it is to be regarded as religion's claim to special knowledge. It can be considered philosophical only in the severely limited sense that philosophers have frequently if not usually granted the possibility of its occurrence. No philosophy that I know of attempts to validate truths reached by revelation. Such an attempt would be a contradiction in terms. Revelation can validate reason's conclusions, but reason can do no more than demonstrate the possibility of revelation's occurring in this kind of world. The general meaning of "revelation" is however quite plain. It is God speaking to man, whether by dreams and visions, as he was thought to do in Old Testament times, or through the church, or through the Sacred Word, or through the sudden indwelling of the Holy Spirit yielding a holy ecstasy. Whatever the medium, the fact of communication *from* God is the distinguishing mark of revelation. The initiative lies with God, not man. There is nothing we can do to bring about a revelation. It licks out of the divine realm with the speed and glory, and sometimes the terror, of summer lightning. Philosophers have usually stayed a respectably safe distance away from such proceedings. Not many of them, even in the seventeenth century, would agree with Francis Bacon's view: "We are obliged to believe the word of God, though our reason be shocked at it. For if we should believe only such things as are agreeable to our reason, we assent to the matter, and not to the author. And therefore, the more absurd and incredible any divine mystery is, the greater honor we do to God in believing it; and so much the more noble the victory of faith." [5]

Whether the Christian faith is entitled to claim special knowledge due to revelation is one of the hotly disputed points in contemporary theological debate, a point on which most of us have pretty definite opinions one way or another. We must not expect much help from philosophy in settling this fuss. In fact those who believe in revelation would not let her help if she tried. They may use more gracious terminology in keeping her out, but it all adds up to this: It's none of her business! If I were a professional philosopher I would be tremendously interested in the progress of the arguments, because the issue is a grave one for philosophy as well as for religion, and I would want to investigate the possibility that religion's appeal to revelation may be related in kind to philosophy's final reliance upon some form of intuition.

To the third query, What do you find in your search for truth? philosophy replies with several different answers. Rationalists — i.e., those who would agree with the Cambridge Platonists that "to follow reason is to follow God " — tell us that mind is the best clue we have to the essential character of reality.   Personalists — i.e., those who would say with Bowne and his disciples, "Personality is the ultimate unit of explanation " — tell us that feeling and will are as truly a part of the basic stuff of the world as is mind.   Empiricists — i.e., those who would say with William James that experience is a collection of heterogeneous facts — are sure to be very modest in their report.   They discover certain unities in areas of fact, but refuse to generalize therefrom to the nature of the universe.   As Professor T. V. Smith once said, " reality is one size too large for the human mind to fit." [6]   But even this doughty warrior will take sides on a moral issue and fight as though it really matters which side wins.   By his actions Professor Smith agrees with William James that in the moment of moral choice we have our deepest dealings with the universe.

Let me summarize in the very briefest way what religion can learn — indeed has learned — from this ancient and exceedingly rich philosophic search for truth.

1.   Religion has not always learned new truths, but she has gained a new confidence in old ones, and this, I suppose, amounts almost to the same thing.   Religion has gained a renewed appreciation of her ancient affirmation as to the mysterious character of the world.   Half of religion's quarrels with philosophy have been occasioned when lesser philosophers pretended to know it all about the world.   But the great traditions in philosophy have begun and ended in the kind of creative wonder which Aristotle asserts to be the mother of philosophy.   The argument from miracle was criticized in religion long before Hume pitched on to it with such devastating force.   But what he did was to make clear that reliance upon argument from miracle is utterly dangerous to the

whole case of religion. Philosophy has aided religion to combat the excesses which grew out of the notion of moral depravity, helping her toward a new confidence in human nature as possessing some very real potentialities for good.

2. Religion has learned to accept the universe as being
essentially reliable. Why there should be some elements of
unreliability in it is a problem that has perplexed and continues to perplex philosophy and religion alike. Religion tends
to charge this unreliability off to sin and philosophy to lack
of integration of experience — which may mean, in a rudimentary way, the same thing. Under the impact of philosophy the factual basis disappeared from underneath such
concepts as devils, demons and angels.[7] But, be it noted, the
accepted reality of truth, beauty and goodness provided the
factual basis for affirming the idea of God. We owe philosophy more than we can imagine for the way in which she has
kept the idea of God geared in with our growing body of
facts garnered from science, art, and human experience generally. It might be overstating the matter to say that she rescued God from the clutches of the ecclesiastics, but it is too
close to the truth for comfort.

3. Under the tutelage of philosophy religion learned to
respect the mind and its function, reason, as an indispensable,
a divinely created instrument for reaching truth. Although
mystical religion has repeatedly sought to minimize the usefulness of mind and reason in the service of God, philosophical religion has steadily insisted that — paraphrasing Shakespeare's line about nature — "reason is made better by no
mean save reason make that mean." This regard for reason
does not rule out the proper exercise of faith; nor could it,
even if it so desired, bring to an end the richness of mystical
insight. But it does place in the hands of man a steady, more
or less reliable instrument with which he can work out his
own salvation, always with fear and trembling. Reason, as
Dr. Reinhold Niebuhr never tires of reminding us, can be in-
fected with pride and can be an instrument in our own de-

struction. This of course is true. But the same can be said of faith, or even of revelation. That reason can be misused is not news to philosophy. Descartes observed, as had Cicero before him, " I had become aware, even so early as during my college days, that no opinion, however absurd and incredible, can be imagined, which has not been maintained by some one of the philosophers." [8]

4.   Finally, religion has learned that she can live with some philosophies but not with others on peril of her soul. She has learned that, by and large, she can live creatively with Platonism, Aristotelianism, Neo-Platonism, and with various forms of idealistic rationalism, personalism and humanistic pragmatism which have grown up in the modern era. Religion has never been able to take these whole. Both she and philosophy have had to go through a process of mutual modification. Sometimes this has helped, sometimes it has weakened religion. For example, Schleiermacher lived in the day when the Romantic movement, with its emphasis upon the primacy of feeling and will, was dominating philosophic thought at least on the continent of Europe. Deeply influenced by it, he developed the theory that the essence of religion is the feeling of absolute dependence upon the universe. While this emphasis rescued religion from the aridities of rationalism, it did so by incurring the dangers of subjectivism, from which later thinkers in turn have had to rescue religion. But the point I want to make is that Schleiermacher's influence, in the historical moment when it occurred, was all to the good, even though it later grew into a distorted emphasis. We need to keep in mind that no philosophical system is a made-to-order ally of religion; if it were, there would be no difference between it and a religion. But some philosophic systems and insights are intrinsically congenial to religion, and upon these religion relies in days of strife and confusion.

There are however, as I have said, types of philosophy with which religion cannot afford to have an intellectual alliance. One such is the kind of mechanistic materialism which swept over Europe in the wake of the Copernican-Newtonian revolution — the idea that the fundamental formula for existence is "mass in motion." This amounts to a denial of cosmic purpose or will, a denial of the reality of spirit, a denial in fact of the ultimacy of any quality or value, because everything can be finally explained in terms of mass in motion. Thomas Hobbes tried not to admit that he accepted this version of reality, but the evidence that he did accept it is clear not only to us who study his *Leviathan;* it was equally clear to his contemporaries. The Cambridge Platonists saw that there is no place for religion in that kind of world; hence they challenged Hobbes with everything in the book of religious and philosophical experience.

Another kind of philosophy which threatens the soul of religion is typified by the wild, heaving voluntarism of Schopenhauer. I say this with the full realization that Schopenhauer's emphasis upon the primacy of will more than counterbalanced Hegel's overemphasis upon reason, to which it was a reaction. But I submit that the Christian religion is sworn to do battle with any view of the world which adds up to this appraisal of human life: "The life of most men is but a continuous struggle for existence — a struggle which they are bound to lose at last. Every breath we draw is a protest against the death which is constantly threatening us, and against which we are battling every second. But Death must conquer after all, for we are his by birth, and he simply plays with his prey a little while longer before devouring it. We, however, take great pains to prolong our lives as far as we can, just as we blow soap bubbles as long and as large as we can, though we know with absolute certainty that they must break at last. . . . The life of most men is weary yearning and torture, a dreamy tottering through the four ages toward death, accompanied by a succession of trivial thoughts. It is like a clockwork that is wound up and goes without knowing why; and every time a man is conceived and born, the clock of human life is wound up anew, in order to grind out the same old hackneyed tune which it has played so many countless times before, measure for measure, beat for beat, with insignificant variations." [9]   No one can deny that Schopenhauer is telling a great many truths in these eloquent passages, but it is the contention of Christian experience that he puts these truths together in such a way as to tell one big lie about life, history and the universe.   His polite bows to religion (and he made some graceful ones) did not deceive many of his contemporaries; they knew that he and the great tradition in religion were moving in opposite directions.

A few years ago an American philosopher, E. S. Spaulding, published a book entitled, *A World of Chance,*[10] which outlines a philosophy equally antithetical to the steadiest affirmations of the Christian faith.   For Spaulding this world is characterized by small associations of units ruled by the iron law of necessary connection — a molecule or cell or galaxy, for example — without there being anything but chance connections obtaining among and between these associations. There is no "universe," no oneness, no wholeness to existence.   Nothing akin to cosmic purpose or direction is known or admissible.   Any notion of value, of truth, beauty, goodness and love, is difficult to retain in such a world view.   As a reminder of the limited character of our knowledge it serves religion well, but as a view of the world it must be rejected by a vital religion.

Let me make this point clear in closing.   I am not saying that the fact that these philosophies are at variance with the Christian religion is necessarily a judgment that they are false and it is true.   That may not turn out to be the case.   All I am saying is this: If they are true, then religion — classical, historical religion — is false.   But for every philosophical system like those last mentioned there are scores that are fundamentally sympathetic with the essential world view of the Christian faith.   It could hardly be otherwise, considering the fact that for most of the past two thousand years philosophy and religion have grown up together in the Western world.

REFERENCES

[1] Phil. 4:8.

[2] Cor. 1:9a (American Translation).

[3] "With whom is no variableness, neither shadow of turning."

[4] Jacques Maritain, *The Angelic Doctor* (New York: Longmans, Green & Co., 1931), p. 24.

[5] Francis Bacon, *De Augmentis,* Book ix.

[6] In an unpublished class lecture.

[7] Not however for Thomas Aquinas, who advances a subtle but finally unconvincing and unnecessary demonology and angelology.

[8] Descartes, *Discourses,* Part II.

[9] Quoted by Frank Thilly, *History of Philosophy* (New York: Henry Holt & Co., 1914), pp. 488–89.

[10] E. S. Spaulding, *A World of Chance* (New York: The Macmillan Co., 1936).

The Greek saw this world almost only on its side of Beauty. His name for it was Cosmos, definite order or regularity. He looked at actions in the same way. One and the same adjective expressed the noble and the beautiful. If he wanted to express the perfect man, he called him a musical or harmonious man.

FREDERICK W. ROBERTSON — *Sermons*

The Richness of Beauty

OUR CONSIDERATION of the philosophical heritage of the Christian faith was undertaken, you may recall, for two main reasons: (1) To remind us that we have a time- and thought- and life-tested gospel to match against the hysterics of the hour in which we must work. We are not called upon to brew some special spiritual magic that can transport our people out of the tragic realities of the day much as opium is reputed to do for its addicts. We preach Jesus Christ as our clearest revelation of God; and we preach this gospel with increased confidence when we realize that it has come to us through some of the richest lives and keenest minds that have arisen in the Western world over nearly two thousand years. (2) To strengthen our flagging faith in our task by the realization that the Christian religion has grown to greatness over many generations, not a few of which lived in a day that was as chaotic for them as ours is for us. We meet the problems of the day with a problem-tested faith, whose relevance now is due in no small measure to the catholicity of the experiences that have gone into its history.

In our first meeting together we tried to get a sort of over-all view of the general relations between religion and philosophy. Since the period when the Christian cult overflowed Judaism and invaded the culture of the rest of the Mediterranean world they have become increasingly interdependent. Plato and Aristotle have furnished the intellectual framework of classical Christian thought. While no one cares to wax dogmatic in these matters, their influence seems at least to equal any that came from the Hebraic tradition. But they are not the only philosophers to leave their mark on the Christian tradition which we seek to mediate week after week to our people. Every great mind in the Western world has made its impression — Descartes, Locke, Hume, Kant, Lotze, Whitehead, to name only a few of the more widely known ones. Philosophers of religion and theologians have had to come to terms with what these men felt to be of greatest truth and importance in the human enterprise. In almost every case our religious tradition has been enriched by this necessity.

We examined next in some detail that portion of our philosophical heritage which centers in the concept of truth. While philosophy said it in its own way, we found reason to believe that there is a solid basis in intellectual fact for Paul's confidence that " God can be depended upon." Philosophy makes use of skepticism, even as religion does, but it is not a skeptical discipline. It is a critical, speculative, rational discipline. It recognizes our overwhelming ignorance and seeks to develop ways of reducing it. Naturally it must rely upon science for most of its information about the universe. I say " most " advisedly because, as we shall see today, philosophers are paying increasing attention to the artist's report on the character and nature of reality. The insights of religion have been almost as influential in philosophy in the Western world as philosophy has been in religion.

But when the philosopher has gathered these various reports on reality from the scientist, the artist and the prophet, his work has just begun. First he must test their validity by whatever standard of truth he believes to be valid. Then he must think them together, see the whole of which they are parts, and construct the outline of a world view — if he can. And finally he must socialize — i.e., put in sharable, useful form — that world view, since it becomes his contribution toward the enrichment of the human enterprise. Religion owes philosophy a debt of incalculable proportions. Not only has philosophy helped us get rid of many of our erroneous notions; she has renewed our confidence in many ideas, beliefs and ideals which have a long religious ancestry. She has helped us purge our idea of God of many of its anthropomorphic qualities. She fought to control the ravages that the notion of the depravity of human nature let loose in religion and in human affairs generally. She has helped us believe in the essential dependability of the universe, of reason and of human nature.

The theme of today's lecture is "The Richness of Beauty." It suggests, to me at least, one of the loveliest of all biblical phrases: "Worship the Lord in the beauty of holiness." This excellent advice springs from the psalmist's perception of the worth and meaning of beauty as well as of holiness. It is — again in my judgment — the supreme description of holiness that we find in the Bible. Nor do I know of a better one in any other body of literature. "The beauty of holiness" is much more meaningful than "the mystery of holiness," largely because it seems to invest holiness with warmth, with a kind of near-at-handness. It does not strip God of mystery but it does suggest the sense of at-homeness in the universe which is truly a part of any profound religious experience. It suggests the joy of being alive, of being allowed to work, to worry and to measure up to one's responsibilities. I cannot believe, therefore, that it is either accidental or incidental advice when we are urged to "worship the Lord in the beauty of holiness."

The modern world has some peculiarly unfortunate ways of accenting, if not separating, this invitation. Some persons appear to want to shorten it until it reads: "Worship the Lord in beauty." While this cannot be considered wholly misleading advice, it must be obvious to everyone that such a view leads to ethical superficiality, largely because it is rooted in metaphysical nonsense. This is a harsh word, I know, but the idea of God as it has slowly taken form in human history and thought includes much more than beauty, however elastically you define that term. Job knew that when he referred to the Almighty as a "Terror." Whitehead knew it when he said that one stage in man's relationship to God almost inevitably is that of "God the Enemy." I have no quarrel with one who believes that beauty may well be our deepest insight into the character of the divine purpose, though I think that such a person usually means by beauty what the Christian faith means by love. But simply to say that "God is all that's beautiful in the world," and stop there, smacks too much of Pippa or Pollyanna. When you separate beauty from the other attributes of God and then proceed to exalt it above them, know it for a fact that ethical storm-signals will soon be flying. Byron, Shelley and Wilde agree with Emerson that "beauty is its own excuse for being," and what an ethical figure they cut! I confess to a growing uneasiness when I study the trend in contemporary churches to "concentrate on lovely worship services," as one minister put it a few months ago. I would not speak one word in derogation of that effort — if it is a part of other efforts; but I would feel much happier about the situation if I did not suspect that what he means by a lovely service is what I mean by an esthetic storm cellar. Beauty is a part of the wholeness of God, and it is our privilege as it is our responsibility to see and celebrate the whole.

On the other hand, some of our contemporary religious leaders appear to drop beauty out of the psalmist's advice and amend it to read: "Worship the Lord in holiness." Rudolph Otto in his well known book, *The Idea of the Holy,* seems to do this. He drops out, as being inadequate, attributes like beauty, goodness, truth, and confronts us with the single stark fact of holiness. In so far as this procedure emphasizes the essentially mysterious character of God there can be no extended quarrel with it. But it is not yet proved that we detract from the mystery and majesty of God when we say, "The Lord is good; his mercy endureth forever," any more than when we affirm, "Holiness belongeth to God."

What I should like to do today is point out the reasons for

believing that one of the essential tasks of religion is to get a clearer understanding of the meaning of beauty and to study the proper mode of celebrating it as an attribute of God. I am fully aware, as you are, of the fact that for many years early Christianity held a strong prejudice, inherited from Judaism, against the use of certain art forms. This applied largely to pictures or images of persons or to attempts to fashion likenesses of deity. The age-old antipathy to idol worship explains this prejudice. It certainly did not extend to other art forms like architecture and music. Nor did the proscription of ikons and idols last long, as their abundance and antiquity testify. It is safe to say that now the Christian is hospitable to practically all art forms, including modern ones like the motion picture. Artists have gained much of their inspiration as well as much of their financial support from the Christian tradition. During the Renaissance, art, like philosophy, set up housekeeping for herself and began to be concerned with the total range of human life.

Esthetics is the study of the beautiful, and it is to this that we turn now. Esthetics is the borderland between art and philosophy, where the speculative artist and the artistically minded thinker seek a clearer understanding of their common interests. Many authentic artists in the mediums of paint and stone have scorned the request to explain in words what they do. Michelangelo said, "I criticize by creating." A contemporary American painter — Thomas Benton, I think it was — declared himself highly suspicious of every effort to convey meanings by words, because words are so indefinite, so ambiguous, and insisted that the artist who says his say through line and color has said it in definite and unambiguous fashion. Notwithstanding this honorable dissent from the usefulness of esthetics, which amounts to a study of the beautiful as recorded in words, a rather voluminous literature on the subject has grown up of late. Notable among these books are Flaccus' *The Spirit and Substance of Art*,[1] which is an excellent introduction to the field; Prall's *Aesthetic Judgment*,[2] which is a much stiffer work; and, of recent date, Horace Kallen's two-volume study entitled *Art and Freedom*.[3] This last is a splendid work which shows a remarkable mastery of the relationship of art to thought and life, but it is unfortunately marred by much fundamental ignorance in matters of religion. But we shall be the poorer if we let that weakness keep us from profiting by its very real strength. I wish more artists would attempt to interpret their work, but they, like scientists, are probably so busy creating it that they have no time to interpret it in other forms. Anyway that is one of the many tasks of philosophy. That is why esthetics is a branch of philosophy.

Philosophers have frequently shared Plato's ambiguous attitude toward art. He did not trust the artist, principally the poet. In the *Republic* he reaches the conclusion that the poet should be permitted to write only under close censorship. Why? Because by his songs and rhymes he can bring the gods and the leaders among men into disrepute. Plato felt that Homer and other poets had definitely debased the deities that had formerly been revered. It is plain that Plato feared the power of the poet and decided that he was too much of a potential menace to be allowed to do as he pleased. This, I submit, is not a very auspicious approach to esthetics. But on the other hand I suppose few philosophers have made as constant use of esthetic insights as did Plato. He labels the supreme vision which is vouchsafed the philosopher as the vision of a "sea of beauty." He regularly makes use of the arts of the craftsman to illustrate the manner in which Ideas form, fashion or control the growth of material substances. In the crowning speech of the *Symposium*, beauty is treated with almost reverent respect. In the *Timaeus*, God, the Creator, is the Cosmic Artist working with tested esthetic forms or patterns in the making of the universe. Professor Kallen epitomizes Plato's conception of beauty thus: ". . . there exists a Beauty absolute, supreme, eternal, one, the begetter and sustainer of the many lesser beauties of beautiful things, which change and perish and deceive; a Beauty real where these are shadows, all-powerful where these are impotent, the sole true goal of man's aspiring love. All existence is but an Art which gives Expression to this ineffable Beauty, all birth and growth is but an endeavor to win back its utterness. It is the heart of the world and the soul of all living." [4]

Both Plato and Aristotle were close students of dramatic art, Aristotle writing a treatise on the art of poetry which continues to be an excellent analysis of the meaning of tragedy. The lineal descendants of these men in the field of thought have paid similar attention to the meaning of art and the work of the artist. Practically every philosopher who has attempted to build his thought along all-inclusive lines has paid careful attention to art. Kant, Schelling, Hegel, Croce and John Dewey may be cited as examples. Professor Charles Hartshorne of the University of Chicago in his book, *Man's Vision of God*, gives this as the reason why philosophy must take note of esthetics: "Aesthetics is the study which has finally brought philosophy to take feeling and quality seriously as positive excellences, not defects. It is time we incorporated this insight into our speculations about God." [5]

Art is variously defined but almost always in terms of beauty. It has been described as "the spontaneous yet disciplined expression of Beauty." Thomas Mann writes, "Art is the most beautiful, the most pungent, the most joyous and the most reverent of symbols for all man's super-rational striving toward the good, toward truth and toward perfection." [6] This incisive definition from the pen of one of the creative artists of our day suggests that the careful study of art is one of the major responsibilities of ministers as well as of philosophers. For we are definitely concerned with any symbol or combination of symbols that will help mankind in the struggle toward the good, toward truth, toward perfection. It is of supreme importance to remember that great art is not created in any studio. The studio has its uses, but the plain fact is that the roots of art are in the common life. Professor Kallen puts the matter in proper perspective when he writes, " When Beauty became a recorded idea as well as an experienced event, and Art a subject for discourse as well as a skilled performance in making over the natural scene, men had been practicing and perfecting this skill for tens of thousands of years." [7]   John Ruskin would agree: " Every herb and flower of the field has its specific, distinct and perfect beauty; it has its peculiar habitation, experience, function. The highest art is that which seizes the specific character, which develops and illustrates it, which assigns to it its proper position in the landscape, and which, by means of it, enhances and enforces the great impression which the picture is intended to convey." [8]   Another student of art writes: " Art reflects deeplying, persistent, ever-actively sought human values; it is one of man's ways of taking and reshaping his world." [9]   Yet art is not purely a practical interest, argued the late Henri Bergson. " The truth achieved by art does not vie with but is superior to the truth of science because art frees our vision from practical interests and conventional modes of apperceptions of objects, and so reveals their unique quality." [10]   Sherwood Anderson, the American writer, attributed art to the life of the imagination: " The life of the imagination will always remain separated from the life of reality. It feeds upon the life of reality, but it is not that life — cannot be. . . . For some reason I myself have never understood very clearly, . . . the imagination must constantly feed upon reality or starve. Separate yourself too much from life and you may at moments be a lyrical poet, but you are not an artist. Something within dries up for the want of food." [11]

Out of this variety of appraisals of art and the artist certain general impressions emerge: (1) Art is practical in that it is an essential part of the human enterprise. (2) Art offers a wider, deeper view of reality than that found in science, but it in no wise supplants or contradicts science. (3) Art is an attempt to create symbols that will enable us to appreciate the reality of the unknown or unappreciated meanings which surround us. (4) The artist, like the early Christian, must be in the world but not of it in that his peculiar contribution comes from his perception of meanings, values and facts which are not items in the body of common appreciations.

It is hard to get an artist to say what beauty means to him. He will usually admit that he is seeking to achieve it, though many contemporary artists would insist with great vigor that they serve truth rather than beauty. The artist Denman Rose somewhere says, "We aim at order and hope for beauty." Other artists would want to paraphrase this to read, "We aim at truth and hope for beauty." Both these statements bring us one step nearer to an understanding of the nature of beauty. For Plato, beauty is the kind of order which issues in symmetrical line, harmonious sound and pleasing pattern. Like all Greek philosophers he hated ugly things, things that were asymmetrical, sounds that jangled or were out of harmony, a life that was out of control of reason, purpose and proportion. "He taught Beauty as the Idea of the Ideas, the living organism which is their unity and the perfect model of such beauty and order as we find in the workaday world. The agencies wherewith God created this world, he taught, were number, harmony, and proportion. . . . God by their means gives shape to the void; of their substance he compounds the elements and establishes Time as the moving image of eternity." [12]

Plato's thinking on the matter of beauty is of a piece with his general philosophical view of the ultimacy of Ideas. Just as an individual man is human because he instances a universal essence of human nature, so also a beautiful vase is beautiful because it instances a universal essence of beauty. As this celestial form or Idea is the controlling or dominating factor in the development of either a life or some created thing of plastic materials, we shall perceive that it is beautiful.

Although Plato seems never to have permitted the separation between concrete object and creative Idea to be made, insisting that they be kept together in the act of thought, the possibility of making such a separation is all too obvious. Aristotle saw it and sought to make them inseparable, but it is doubtful whether he made any appreciable advance over Plato in this regard.   Plotinus, whose life was lived in a world that was definitely out of control of human reason and planning, saw and exploited the possibility of the separation.   He developed the idea that beauty is one of the most powerful formative forces in the universe; that the artist is its creature; that it bestows upon beautiful objects something of its essence, hence their beauty, but they in no wise do more than merely suggest its nature.   For him, beauty comes to be the only real thing in a world of transient facts.   Hence let the world of change and decay go its own way while the man of wisdom worships at the shrine of imperishable beauty.   Plotinus gives to all life an esthetic vocation — that of searching for beauty, of seeking to become the embodiment of as much beauty as possible.   To do this is to be most deeply in tune with the Infinite, the One, who is the spiritual Unity in existence.   He can account for the profound impression which a beautiful object makes on the human spirit only by arguing that "the soul includes a faculty peculiarly addressed to Beauty, one incomparably sure in the appreciation of its own, never in doubt when any lovely thing presents itself for judgment." [13]   This, of course, goes far beyond anything that Plato or Aristotle suggested, but it is safe to say that it represents one of the most frequently used ideas of Plotinus.

Before Augustine became a Christian — almost certainly while he was an enthusiastic Neo-Platonist — he wrote a treatise on esthetics which bore the title, *De apto et pulchro,* "The Fit and the Beautiful."   It is symbolic of the predominantly moral climate of the early Christian church that we do not have a copy of this book; in fact, our only knowledge of it comes from Augustine's celebrated *Confessions.*   The author was ashamed of having written it because it dealt with

" lines, and colors and masses," and in no wise celebrated the glory of God as revealed in Jesus Christ. But, as Mr. Kallen points out, Augustine is not a person to regret an inconsistency. His interest in art and the beautiful keeps coming to the surface in his other and supposedly more Christian writings. Like Plotinus he finds the only adequate explanation of earthly beauty in the reality of " the sublimated essence of Beauty, which is heavenly Beauty." [14]

Augustine seems to have dipped pretty deeply into numerology, the belief that numbers possess some mystical quality. Number is the symbol of order, of measurement and proportion; hence it must be closely related to the internal structure of beauty, both earthly and heavenly. God and the artist alike create beautiful objects according to law or proportion, with this difference, that " God makes his creations by fiat out of nothing, men must work on matter. They take such materials as language, marble, ivory, and model them in the numbers and forms which are innate to their own souls and bodies. . . . The nature of music makes it aptest to express man's own inner harmony and his fittest instrument to worship God with. By living the beautiful we live for God and with our aspirations move toward him. Beauty is a way, revealed by faith, to ineffable God." [15]

It is hard for me to see that Thomas Aquinas added anything new to the esthetic conceptions which prevailed in his time, though he did infuse Aristotle's matter-of-fact discussions with something of the glow of Plotinus and Augustine. Beauty he believed to be the " harmony of differences." Of course he puts it in his own awkward but amazingly exact way: ". . . as for beauty of body, a certain fit proportion of members and color superadded is necessary, without which there is no beauty; so for beauty universally: to the proportion of parts and of the whole there must be added a certain *claritas formae* (clarifying form). . . . Beauty does not consist of its components as a thing does but in a certain outshining of form — *resplendentia formae*. In this effulgence of form is to be found the specific differentiation wherein the principle of the beautiful is manifest." [16]   When Aquinas speaks of the " harmony of differences " he seems to mean by harmony a certain sense of inner fitness or, as we might say, of wholeness, of belonging together.   One temperamentally so at variance with him as George Eliot could agree that the maximum of beauty is achieved when the largest number of possible variants has been worked into one coherent whole. Quoting Dr. Hartshorne again: " Let there be as much unity in contrast as possible, both within the new pattern and between it and the old patterns — so that the pattern of ongoing life shall be unified and diversified. . . . This is the esthetic imperative which the artist feels laid upon him by the scheme of things, and it is the voice of God as truly as any other imperative." [17]

To go back to our historical sketch for one more moment: Following, and concluding, the Middle Ages three groundswells swept through Western culture and left nothing unchanged.   I refer to the Renaissance, the Enlightenment, and the age of Romanticism.   Our present purpose requires that we trace the course of esthetics, or the emphasis upon beauty, through these periods.

The Renaissance, coming as it did at the close of the great period of Scholasticism, was not the clean break with the past which we too frequently think it.   It did compromise the authority of the church; it did challenge the all-sufficiency of faith and dogma in matters of ultimate truth; but it did not disclaim authority nor did it reject religion.   It proclaimed the authority of the culture of the ancients, principally the Greeks, and it emphasized the humane values in religion. The Renaissance meant a turning away from the kind of otherworldliness which had become traditional in religion, and which had a strong taproot in the philosophy of Plato, especially as interpreted by Plotinus.   Looking at the human enterprise through the eyes of the warm-blooded Greeks and Romans was a new experience to persons who had become accustomed to viewing it through the eyes of Christian doctrine as interpreted by monks. They discovered the goodness of man, of life, of the earth, of human society. Life became something to be affirmed, not denied. Although the greatest artists of the Renaissance — Leonardo da Vinci, Michelangelo, Raphael — never strayed far from religious subjects for their creations, they handled them with a new freedom and appreciation. Leonardo's horses all but spring off the canvas and the pedestal. Michelangelo's men have been caught in the grip of some gigantic stress; their full-muscled bodies are taut with emotion. Even Raphael, the most ethereal of the three, brings into his women and children a humanness that is always startling. By and large, the Renaissance did not deny the reality of beauty; rather it sought it with greater freedom in this world, in terms of the struggles and beauties of this life. With Petrarch and Dante poetry put on the garb of the common tongues and began to sing of the common life. It is perhaps fair to sum the matter up by saying that, owing to the Renaissance, art became less rational and ecclesiastical and more human both in spirit and in technique.

"Enlightenment" denotes that extraordinary epoch in our cultural tradition when man was supremely confident of himself and of his world. The pendulum had swung to the other pole from that of the medieval world. Then man was afraid of this world; he mistrusted his powers and abilities; he denied the goodness of his body and worried steadily over the eternal abode of his soul. The Renaissance represents midpoint in the pendulum's swing to the other extreme. But the swing went on, under the impetus of the emerging world of science. The work of Copernicus, Galileo, Newton, coupled with the philosophy of Descartes, Bacon, Hobbes, gave man a radically different view of the world in which he lived. In place of a mystery he was given a machine. He was persuaded that science could master the running of the machine and that "knowledge is power." The great day of rationalism dawned with its extravagant eulogies of reason and man and its incredible hopes for an increasingly serene future for mankind.

But it was not a happy world in spite of the many philosophical panegyrics that were written. Professor E. A. Burtt gives us this description of it: " It was of the greatest consequence for succeeding thought that now the great Newton's authority was squarely behind that view of the cosmos which saw in man a puny, irrelevant spectator (so far as a being wholly imprisoned in a dark room can be called such) of the vast mathematical system whose regular motions according to mechanical principles constituted the world of nature. . . . The world that people had thought themselves living in — a world rich with colour and sound . . . speaking everywhere of purposive harmony and creative ideals — was crowded now into minute corners in the brains of scattered organic beings. The really important world outside was a world, hard, cold, colourless, silent and dead — a world of quantity, a world of mathematically computable motions in mechanical regularity. The world of qualities as immediately perceived by man became just a curious and quite minor effect of that infinite machine, beyond. In Newton, the Cartesian metaphysics, ambiguously interpreted and stripped of its distinctive claim for serious philosophical consideration, finally overthrew Aristotelianism, and became the predominant world-view of modern times." [18]

Needless to say, artists had to fight for their souls in a day which thought it lived in a world like this. As a matter of fact this struggle seems to have been good for many of them. Shakespeare wrote in the early part of the seventeenth century and Milton about the middle of it. But Professor Basil Willey is of the opinion that both these men blandly refused to be cowed by the mechanical pretensions of their age. They had meat to eat that their contemporaries knew not of. Shakespeare lived at the end of that glorious Elizabethan period which drew much of its inspiration from the Italian Renaissance. Milton's work " is much like an isolated volcano thrusting up through the philosophic plains, and drawing its fire from deeper and older levels of spiritual energy. . . . He lived in a moral rather than a physical world, and was ready to imbibe wisdom wherever he could find it." [19]   But, except where artists deliberately set their face against the accepted interpretation of the world, as did Shakespeare and Milton, it was a sorry time for them to live and try to work in.   Beauty was no longer fundamental; it was scarcely skin deep.   In fact it was commonly regarded as a cheat and a liar because it talked about things that were " scientifically " untrue.   Although some of the greatest leaders in this intellectual revolution — men like Francis Bacon, Descartes, Hobbes and John Locke — professed to hold and — let us give them credit — did hold the Bible in veneration as the repository of revealed truth, there was such an actual discrepancy between it and their philosophic world view that the obvious conflict required constant explanation on their part and that of some of their contemporaries, like Sir Thomas Browne.   Religion fared as ill as poetry and the other arts.   Like them it simply could not exist in the mathematically precise yet actually soulless world of which the devotees of the new science were speaking.

It was in this " evil time " that the Cambridge Platonists, to whom we have repeatedly referred, came forward with a forthright challenge to the validity of the prevalent materialism.   Significantly enough, great art and vital religion stand or fall together.   The forces which imperil one threaten the other; whatever aids one strengthens both.   We have no sure way of measuring the influence of these latter-day disciples of Plato.   It is enough to note the fact that by their protest they set in motion a tremendous debate which, at minimum, kept the mechanists from sealing up the jar of human creativity. As long as the issue was in doubt the courageous artist could choose to believe in the world as mystery rather than machine, could serve beauty in the catacombs, if need be.

The whole Romantic movement can best be regarded as

the protest of the esthetic and religious conscience against the superficiality of the mechanistic world view which science and philosophy had attempted to saddle on the human spirit. Hume helped pave the way for the protest when, early in the eighteenth century, he took the whole notion of causality, the crucial point in the mechanistic world view, under heavy logical and psychological fire. At the same time Rousseau was demanding to know how feeling and will could be so easily ignored by any factually grounded philosophy; he insisted that they are faculties of equal importance with reason, if not of greater importance.

Immanuel Kant was determined to have it both ways and so set about constructing a theory of knowledge and reality which would make room for mechanistic science and vital religion alike. There are, he argued, two worlds: the noumenal and the phenomenal. The phenomenal is the world as mediated through sensation, and is therefore the area where rigorous law prevails. In this world science has not only the last but also the only word in regard to truth. The noumenal world is "the real world as opposed to the appearance world." [20] Although it cannot be known, its existence must be postulated by the practical reason; that is, it must be *there* for sensations and knowledge to be even possible. Since sensation and knowledge are indubitable, the noumenal world too is indubitable, even though unknown. Understanding and knowledge have meaning only when kept close to the empirical data of experience; since none of these brings us more than a fragment of reality we are unable to say that we know anything about the essential character or nature of the real world, the world which is the source of our experience. While denying that we can erect grandiose metaphysical systems, after the fashion of Plato and Aristotle, Kant felt that such tremendous realities as God, immortality and freedom may safely be affirmed as true since they are inescapable postulates of the practical reason. In other words, we cannot do business in this world without assuming their truth. God guarantees " the moral governance of a world in which virtue is crowned with happiness "; immortality assures us that " the pursuit of moral perfection may continue beyond the empirical life of man "; freedom is the only adequate explanation of the fact that " the will of a rational being is . . . a law unto itself." [21]   Kant proceeds to make way for renewed emphasis upon beauty.   The " esthetic judgment," as he calls it, is probably the clearest insight we have into the reality of the noumenal world.   By means of it we sense, in an indescribable way, the essential relevance of our reason and moral judgments in both worlds.

Following through the opening made by Kant came a whole troop of thinkers who are usually known as the romantic idealists.   They were bent on destroying the mechanistic world view and developing one that made due allowance for feeling, will and intuition.   Schelling and Hegel, each in his own way, developed the Kantian protest.   Poets joined in with great gusto, Goethe and Wordsworth being the most prominent.   The effectiveness of this movement may be gauged by Professor Kallen's judgment that " the establishment of the arts among the vital primacies of life was accomplished in the form of that posture of the spirit of western man which is called Romanticism." [22]   Out of it came such memorable testimonies as those of Wordsworth and Keats:

> " I held unconscious intercourse with beauty
> Old as creation, drinking in a pure
> Organic pleasure from the silver wreaths
> Of curling mist, or from the level plain
> Of waters coloured by impending clouds." [23]

> " A thing of beauty is a joy forever;
> Its loveliness increases; it will never
> Pass into nothingness." [24]

> " Beauty is truth, truth beauty, — that is all
> Ye know on earth, and all ye need to know." [25]

Out of all this grows the overwhelming impression that the human spirit simply refuses to believe that it is living in a world in which beauty is not a profound and true insight into the character of ultimate reality.

Let us now turn from this historical fact and inquire more precisely what it is the artist is trying to do. The materials with which he works will vary from one kind of art to another. Kallen builds his monumental work around the thesis that the manual arts are the fundamental art forms of any culture. This of course does not rule out or minimize the importance of the fine arts, but it does make them conscious of their rugged relatives. Concentrating upon the fine arts for the moment, it is clear that the artist may choose any one of several mediums. He may use color or sound or line or words. Each material requires a special technique which he must learn as best he can. But regardless of the medium, his basic problems are the same: How impose form upon this material? How place it in a significant perspective? How bring out a unity of meaning through it? His initial problem however is: Why do anything with it at all? Why not simply leave it alone? The artist will invariably answer that he wants to do something with it or wants to say something through it. John Keats gives this as his reason for writing: "I feel assured that I should write for the mere yearning and fondness I have for the beautiful even if my night's labors should be burnt every morning and no eye ever shine on them. . . . I value more the privilege of seeing the great things in loneliness than the fame of a prophet." [26] Writing of "the major workmen and their serious followers" among contemporary American artists, Thomas Craven says: "With these draftsmanship is of prime importance; they are more concerned with the anatomy of the human figure and the topography of the landscape than with the appearances of nature at the given moment. Their aim is to get at meanings, to know America, and to design compact structures communicating the poetry and magnificence, the irony, the humor, the shabbiness, the tragedy, and,

not least, the social significance of their chosen materials." [27]
It ought to be a truism that a work of art is not a photograph
and makes no pretense of being one. It is a deliberate abstraction from a whole, the selection of some one aspect or
phase of it. It is at this point that so many of us misunder-
stand the artist. We measure what he does by the total fact
which we see, thus missing the point of his work.

I had the privilege of learning this lesson the hard way a
few years ago when a young artist confronted me with a
sketch of the main spire of our church in Baltimore.[28] While
I appreciated the sketch very much, especially after I learned
that he had spent three months on it, it did seem to leave
something out. When I called his attention to the fact that
one of the subordinate spires was not developed proportionally with the main one he replied, " I wasn't interested in that
one. It was the tall one I was after." Whereupon I pointed
out that certain of the horizontal lines of the main spire
seemed to be indefinite. He answered, " I wasn't after them;
I was after the vertical lines." When I said that the spire was
a lot more than vertical lines he asked, " What do you want?
A photograph of it? " We went out to the spot on which he
had stood while he made the sketch, and I got an exacting lesson in the intention of the artist. Some time later I did get a
photograph of the church and for my own satisfaction laid it
alongside the sketch. The artist had those vertical lines that
he was after, and he had them in proportion and perspective
too.

The fact is that an artist can choose to develop any given
aspect of a scene or object that appeals to him. A photograph of some cows grazing in a meadow will be quite a different thing from an artist's study of the lines of perspective
which govern the relationship of cows, brook, trees and roll-
ing countryside; yet that relationship is as real a factor in the
original scene as the color of the cows or the sheen of the water in the sunlight. You may have heard of Whistler's reply
to the attorney who was cross-questioning him during his

libel suit against Ruskin. Referring to Whistler's painting "Nocturne in Blue and Silver," the attorney wanted to know what it represented. Whistler replied, "That depends on who looks at it." This is much more than simply a tart answer (though Whistler would not have used it if it had not been tart); it is stating the truth that to someone seeking photographic precision in object relations the picture would have been little more than a dull smudge, while to someone interested in the way night softens the shades of colors which are quite distinct in bright light it is a masterly piece of work. It happened that when Whistler created it he was making that kind of study in color, and as such it is superb.

You almost have to see an artist at work to appreciate the enormous amount of effort which goes into the development of detail. Leonardo da Vinci's *Notebook* is a lesson in humility to anyone addicted to tossing off snap judgments on the worth of art creations. When Leonardo began her portrait, "Mona Lisa was something over twenty-four years of age; when she last sat to him she was nearly thirty." [29] The great painter wrote a *Treatise on Painting* which is a full discussion of what the technical problems are and how to meet them. The least we can do is to let the artist tell his own story in his own way. He has chosen as his medium of communication something other than reason and discussion. If after studying his creation we still do not " get " it, it is superfluous to ask him or anyone else to "explain" it. It either says what it has to say or it does not. Why anyone should wish to go beyond that is difficult to see.

We come now, in conclusion, to an enumeration of several very valuable things which religion can learn from art. These are at most simply details in the total and mutual indebtedness which binds these two creative disciplines together.

1.   We can learn to appreciate the richness of concrete fact.[30] We cannot speak about the simplest fact without using some symbol. Any symbol we use, whether word or line, is an abstraction drawn from the rich unity of the whole

fact. Consider the variety of ways in which an airplane in flight can be apprehended. To an engineer in aerodynamics it is mass in motion. To the artist it is a combination of color, sound, motion and a definite pattern in line of design and flight. To the ethicist its cargo, destination and purpose loom as paramount. To the pilot it may be the same old thing, or it may be the exhilarating sensation of being shaken free from earth, of being alone. All are valid perspectives of an airplane in flight; there is no known way in which one can rule the others out as irrelevant or untrue.

One of the surest cures imaginable for individual dogmatism is to learn to appreciate the richness of concrete facts. Anathemas pronounced against persons and ideas may seem to be morally necessary; they are none the less esthetic nonsense. A fact, any fact, must be studied carefully before we make it the basis of judgment. It has both an "esthetic surface" — i.e., the portion that meets the eye and is readily grasped — and its core of meaning — the way in which it fits into some larger whole. The more important a fact is, the harder it is to keep faith with its richness. That is why so much of censorship in art is simply misguided moral enthusiasm, likely to do more harm than good. It is most devoutly to be hoped that God has a sense of humor as he sees our frantic efforts to promote virtue by refusing to face the realities of evil. But then that is an ancient failing of religious folk.

2. The initial step in knowledge is individual awareness. By awareness, the artist means an almost mystical sensation of identification with the object of his attention. Professor DeWitt Parker calls this the amazing capacity of great artists for living themselves into the life around them. George Eliot illustrates it in her testimony: "There are hours when I escape from myself, when I live in a plant, when I feel myself leaf, bird, treetop, wave, running water, color, form . . . when I drink the dew . . . when I expand to the sun . . . when I sleep under the leaves, when I move with the larks and romp with the lizards, when I shine with the stars or the

dazzling worms; when, in short, I live in everything which is a medium of development, which is like a dilation of my being." [31] Tennyson put it much more simply when he wrote: " I am a part of all that I have met." [32] The presently accepted psychological doctrine that interest and desire are precursors of attention are pale reflections of this intense esthetic doctrine of knowledge through identification of the knower with the known. While it is easy to push this view into an absurdity the solid fact remains that the process of knowing involves what the late George Herbert Mead calls " the manipulation of the object " by the mind. This is simply a multiplying of the facets by which we hold it in our attention and memory. In order to get hold of an object of knowledge we must lose ourselves in it. The artist knows this and as the first act in his creation loses himself in the process of seeing the meaning which he intends to try to reproduce in his medium. This is usually the hardest part of the artist's work; its richness and creativity depend upon the range of his experience as well as upon the keenness of his insight into the core of meaning which comes to focus in the object.

This lesson was put in unforgettable terms for religion a long time ago: " Except a corn of wheat fall into the ground and die it abideth alone, but if it die it bringeth forth much fruit "; " He that saveth his life shall lose it, but he that loseth his life for my sake shall save it." Detachment and objectivity have their indispensable part to play in the acquisition of knowledge about atoms and cells. But if we are investigating the phenomena of poverty and inequity we must feel the injustice with the sensitivity of an artist like George Eliot, else we will miss the greatest fact about the object of our search. The only cure for the callousness which is coming to be one of the characteristics of this tragic day is suggested by one of Rembrandt's paintings, " The Raising of the Cross." The artist is trying to say that this man is being put to death by and for the sins of the world. How does he say it? Here is the arrestingly white figure of the Christ on the cross. All around in varying shades of darkness are the other figures — the high priest and his men, the soldiers, the weeping women; and still another figure who is helping the soldiers lift the cross — *Rembrandt himself.* Archbishop Temple puts it nicely: " The man who would see Truth must yield his mind to the facts; the man who would enjoy Beauty must surrender his soul to its spell; the man who would love must give his very self, for that is what love is." [33]

3.   The artist is akin to the prophet and seer in religion. I maintain that there is a difference in degree not in kind between Jeremiah struggling to understand the life of Judah and Walt Whitman interpreting the life of America in " Starting from Paumanok " or " I Hear America Singing." Both Jeremiah and Whitman are trying to interpret the deep things of the divine will as it manifests itself in the spirit of a people in a definite historical epoch. Although Jeremiah is incomparably the greater of the two in every way, Whitman is trying as earnestly as he to interpret the will of God to his people. Both feel impelled to their tremendous tasks; both struggle against the temptation to withdraw from it; both are finally driven by a force which they cannot resist but need not serve into the depths of the life of their people. What Professor Hartshorne has called " the esthetic imperative " is, as he says, " the voice of God as truly as any other imperative," is blood-brother to the prophetic insistence, " The voice of the Lord came unto me."

This fact alone is warrant for a good deal of artistic license. We ought to be as considerate of our artists as we desire them to be of our prophets. To adapt Henry Thoreau's words, they may be stepping to some music that we do not hear. Few artists misuse or abuse the leeway which great art demands. I suppose it is true that the monstrosities and absurdities of art are more numerous than the masterpieces, but one masterpiece can outweigh in importance any number of them. True as this is of art, it is even truer of religion. In this sense, then, tolerance is the only open road to creativity

in art and religion alike. It takes the courage of a Beethoven
to serve beauty austerely. He once said, "There is no rule
that may not be broken for the sake of beauty." [34] I submit
that we need that kind of spirit.

4. The artist has helped us better to appreciate the infinite beauty of God. It is good scriptural doctrine that God
built beauty into the structure of the world. The psalmist
repeatedly bursts out in adoration of the beauty of the heavens. Jesus invited his disciples to consider the lilies of the
field as examples of common but unsurpassable beauty.
Even in Paul, whose moralistic bent is true to his Jewish background, we find intimations of the Greek culture in which
Phidias and others had labored: "Know ye not that ye are
the temple of God, and that the Spirit of God dwelleth in
you?" I maintain that the burden of proof rests upon anyone
who is concerned to deny the Greek ancestry of these senti-
ments. The body of man is formed by his soul or formative
spirit even as an artist molds his materials. Studying "The
Discus Thrower" and "Aphrodite of Cyrene" makes it easier
to understand why the Greeks regarded the body as beautiful, thus paving the way for their belief in the intrinsic beauty
of the distinctively human Idea or Form.

I do not see how anyone can hear some of the great ora-
torios without confessing that they deepen and broaden the
meaning of the scriptural passages that serve as texts. Each
time I hear Stainer's *Crucifixion,* Calvary becomes more a
fact and less an argument. Only the musician can adequately
portray the joy, the melancholy, the triumph and the tragedy
of the human spirit. One of the greatest spiritual pilgrimages
open to anyone is to hear Faure's *Requiem,* which begins in
the gloom and tragedy of death and closes with the soft notes
of a lullaby radiant with peace and love. Art creations like
these are great because they tie into an organic unity moods,
experiences and beliefs which are so widely varied in character that they are usually kept apart. But the artist senses
their intrinsic fitness for and to each other. He puts them to-

gether in such a way that triumph is wrested out of tragedy and hope out of despair. Professor Hartshorne relates works of art to God in this interesting passage: "God is neither a poem containing all possible poems . . . nor is he the mere sum of all actual poems, nor yet merely one poem among others, nor finally is he sheerly above all definite patterns and forms. He is rather the never ending poem of which all actual poems are phrases, all cosmic epochs yet elapsed are verses, and whose 'to be continued' is the promise of infinite poetic creation to come." [35]

One word more about the supreme unity in diversity which constitutes the beauty of God. At least two biblical passages suggest that we are not the first to be arrested by this fact: "The earth is the Lord's and the fullness thereof; the world and they that dwell therein"; and the New Testament passage: "All things work together for good to them that love God." It is not in the least making these verses bear a burden that was not intended to say that they seem to convey some profound appreciation of the almost infinite variety of things, persons and events which either constitute God or belong under his unitive control. This fact points up the fallacy of overabstraction in all our definitions about God; while what they say is important, what they leave out is important too. This is why religion and the arts grew up together. They need each other. They are trying to tell the truth about, to celebrate the beauty of, a common Subject, even God himself. Together they say, "Worship the Lord in the beauty of holiness."

REFERENCES

[1] Louis W. Flaccus, *The Spirit and Substance of Art* (New York: F. S. Crofts & Co., 1926).

[2] D. W. Prall, *Aesthetic Judgment* (New York: Thomas Y. Crowell, 1929).

[3] Horace M. Kallen, *Art and Freedom*, 2 vols. (New York: Duell, Sloane & Pearce, 1942).

[4] *Ibid.*, I, 36.

[5] Charles Hartshorne, *Man's Vision of God* (Chicago: Willett, Clark & Co., 1941), p. 224.

[6] Thomas Mann, Introduction to Tolstoy's *Anna Karenina* (New York: Random House, 1939), p. xxv.

[7] Kallen, *op. cit.*, I, 35.

[8] Quoted *ibid.*, I, 543.

[9] Flaccus, *op. cit.*, p. 5.

[10] As interpreted by DeWitt Parker, *Human Values* (New York: Harper & Brothers, 1931), p. 343.

[11] Sherwood Anderson, *Notebook* (New York: Liveright Publishing Corp., 1926), pp. 72–73. Quoted by Parker, *op. cit.*, p. 351.

[12] Kallen, *op. cit.*, I, 43.

[13] Quoted by Grace Turnbull, *Tongues of Fire* (Baltimore: Johns Hopkins Press, 1941), p. 317.

[14] Kallen, *op. cit.*, I, 85. Also in Grace Turnbull, *The Essence of Plotinus* (New York: Oxford University Press, 1934), pp. 43 ff.

[15] Kallen, *op. cit.*, I, 85–86.

[16] Quoted by Kallen, *ibid.*, I, 108.

[17] Hartshorne, *op. cit.*, p. 229.

[18] E. A. Burtt, *The Metaphysical Foundations of Modern Science* (London: Kegan Paul, Trench, Trubner & Co., Ltd., 1925), pp. 236–37.

[19] Basil Willey, *The Seventeenth Century Background* (New York: Columbia University Press, 1942), pp. 226, 239.

[20] *Dictionary of Philosophy*, edited by D. D. Runes (New York: Alliance Book Corp., 1942), p. 215.

[21] *Ibid.*, p. 159.

[22] Kallen, *op. cit.*, I, 199.

[23] Wordsworth, *The Prelude*, Book I, lines 562–66.

[24] Keats, *Endymion*, Book I, Proem.

[25] Keats, " Ode on a Grecian Urn."

[26] Quoted by Parker, *op. cit.*, p. 325.

[27] Thomas Craven in his Introduction to *A Treasury of American Prints* (New York: Simon & Schuster, 1938).

[28] Mount Vernon Place Methodist Church. The artist is Mr. Alfred E. Reid.

[29] Antonina Vallentin, *Leonardo da Vinci* (New York: Viking Press, 1938), p. 356.

[30] Cf. Prall, *op. cit., passim.*

[31] Quoted by Parker, *op. cit.*, pp. 337–38.

[32] Tennyson, " Ulysses."

[33] Archbishop Temple, *Nature, Man and God* (New York: The Macmillan Co., 1934), p. 518.

[34] Quoted by Parker, *op. cit.*, p. 340.

[35] Hartshorne, *op. cit.*, pp. 226–27.

So wide arms
Hath goodness infinite, that it receives
All who turn to it.

DANTE — *Purgatory*

O give thanks unto the Lord; for he is good: for his mercy endureth for ever.

Psalm 106:1

. IV .

The Strength of Goodness

YOU WILL recall from previous statements of the purpose behind our study of Christianity's philosophical heritage that we are not engaged in a sort of sightseeing tour among the ruins of philosophic systems. While that would be an interesting and perhaps instructive venture it is not what we are trying to do. We are studying some of the various ways in which the insights and emphases of the amazingly rich philosophical tradition of Western civilization have become the intellectual framework of the Christian faith. We do this not so much to be able to give credit where credit is due (though since the Reformation we have tended to slight our theological debt to philosophy), but rather in order that we may be better ministers of Jesus Christ to this troubled day in which we seek to work. At precisely the moment when our historic civilization seems to be sprung at every seam, thus threatening to let in the waters of destruction over us all, it is of utmost necessity that we guard against panic-born and hysteria-freighted utterances. One way of doing this is to get a fresh grip on the fact that our faith is a hard-won, time- and thought-tested achievement. It was born in a gravely critical period; it bears in its body the scars of succeeding eras of confusion, some of which issued in the collapse of the social order. Yet through it all Christianity has maintained a sense of mission and commission. It has brought to our historical tradition an element of permanence that only recently, in the writings of men like Christopher Dawson and Arnold Toynbee, has been receiving adequate recognition. What we are now engaged in is the laying bare of that rugged intellectual framework of our faith which in any fair reckoning must loom as one of the reasons for the greatness of the Christian religion.

The opening lecture was devoted to sketching an over-all picture of the way in which Christian thinkers have more or less consciously fallen back on the classical philosophical tradition stemming principally from Greece and, of course, from the writings of Plato and Aristotle. In the early days of the Christian era many of the most important converts had been steeped in Greek thought before they felt the claim of the new religion. Men like Clement of Alexandria, Justin Martyr and Augustine were already in possession of what was later to become the rational framework of their faith when they entered the Christian church. Such men did not depreciate philosophy (that near-crime was reserved for others); they put it to immediate and good use. In the thirteenth century Thomas Aquinas used the system of Aristotle to bring new order into the increasingly chaotic state of Christian thought and life. Again, in the seventeenth century the Cambridge Platonists, alarmed by the inroads of Hobbes's blatant materialism and by the mechanistic interpretation of life which was being encouraged by emerging science, summoned Plato out of the background and placed him in the foreground of the faith. We did not comment on the rightness or wrongness of this strategy. We simply noted it, and noted also the plain fact that it succeeded in its object; i.e., Christian leaders immediately regained confidence in the intellectual validity of their faith.

The second and third lectures were studies in details of this larger picture. We saw how and why it is erroneous to regard philosophy as an essentially skeptical discipline. We learned to respect the care with which it seeks to keep faith with the fact of our ignorance. We saw that ultimately it affirms the dependability of the world, of reason and of the human enterprise without minimizing the problems to be faced in so doing. Our study of esthetics reminded us of our debt to the artists, who by their labors have helped reveal the manifold richness of reality. Recognition of this fact has rescued philosophy from the very real danger of overemphasizing the method of analysis and abstraction, upon which logic must necessarily rely. We discovered how essential it is to trust the artist with all the freedom he wants, because the dangers we thus incur are less to be feared than those which grow out of an attempt to coerce him into conformity. He has something to teach us about the richness of concrete fact, about the necessity of losing oneself in anything one would understand and interpret, about the meaning of a sensitive, receptive, humble approach to reality.

Today we shall study another detail in the general picture of our philosophical heritage — the strength of goodness. No discussion of the structure of the Christian religion could be considered complete without careful attention to this area. " Cease to do evil; learn to do good," is an apt summary of one of the richest parts of the prophetic literature of Hebraism. Characteristically, the Greek philosophical influence played upon this forthright ethical advice and brought about a rich psychological and rational development of the idea of goodness. The restless Greek genius for asking questions looked at the simple ethical formulas of the Hebrew tradition from every conceivable angle. I do not mean to imply that Greek culture had had no thought of its own about the good and goodness; as we shall see, the reverse was true. One of the major problems of early Christian thinkers was to fuse the best insights of both traditions on this point.

It is always wise to focus our gaze squarely on the fact of goodness before we outline and discuss the theory underlying and explaining it. Mr. A. A. Milne in his play *Michael and Mary* pictures a condition of tension between Michael and his father — one for which both are to blame. They never quite succeed in staying out of each other's way. The father cannot forget that he is the father; he is always ready to help the boy no matter what the trouble is. After one such situation — an especially serious one — Michael says: "There's something about sheer goodness that gets me. Mind you, I disagree with you profoundly about everything under the sun, sometimes you irritate me intensely and — and yet — I believe I love you." [1]   Something of this sheer goodness shines through the pivotal persons in the Jewish-Christian tradition. (Not that it is by any means limited to that tradition!) Looking into our Old Testament, we are struck by the life and faith of Hosea as an example of it. His story is well known to us, but that does not keep it from standing us up very straight each time we read it. As one startled layman said upon hearing it, "That fellow had something I lack!" He had something that most of us lack — the ability to hear and heed the voice of a good God. Another incarnation of goodness in the Old Testament is the "suffering servant" of the Second Isaiah. Whether these passages are about a man or Israel does not much matter; they are moving insights into the tragic character of all true goodness. They also make the unforgettable point that in God's will alone can goodness truly be sought. Jesus Christ has been the supreme example of goodness to Christians. His Sermon on the Mount is, as it were, his last will and testament to subsequent generations. Who can read it without finding his own life and works under the judgment of a good God?   St. Francis of Assisi exemplifies a peculiar yet winsome form of undebatable goodness. Taylor writes of him in *The Medieval Mind:* "Francis' life was not compassed by its circumstances nor was its effect limited to the thirteenth century. His life partook of the eternal, and might move men in times to come as simply and directly as it turned men's hearts to love in the years when Francis was treading the rough stones of Assisi." [2]   I should like to include the name of the early American Quaker, John Woolman, in this list of persons who come to mind when sheer goodness is mentioned. Of him, no less vigorous a social realist than the late Arthur Holt said that five hundred John Woolmans mov-

ing about in the colonies would have solved the problem of
slavery and thus obviated the Civil War — and, lest we forget, the recent riots in Detroit and other places.

Our further procedure in this hour will parallel that of
earlier lectures: We shall study with some care the various
notions of the good and goodness that have become a part of
our philosophic and religious tradition. We shall then determine whether there are significant elements held in common
by them which may yield a more definite notion of the meaning of good and goodness. Finally we shall inquire into the
implications of this investigation for religion. We take this
line without losing sympathy with Thomas à Kempis' dictum,
" I had rather know compunction than its definition." It is
just possible that knowledge of the possible meaning of goodness will not preclude — may even enrich — the experience
of it.

We no sooner turn to a survey of the various notions that
have been advanced as defining the good and goodness than
we encounter an embarrassment of riches. Even Augustine,
in the year 400, records the fact that he is troubled by infinite
variety in this field. He says that a certain Varro has been
able to enumerate two hundred and eighty-eight different
conceptions of the highest good. It is hard not to believe that
at least another hundred have been added in the last fifteen
hundred years. We must learn to be patient in the presence
of such variety. It isn't as scandalous as it sounds. It is our
surest guarantee that the idea or problem under description
and definition is of admitted importance. Men do not spend
that much time on something that does not matter much one
way or another. To say this is not to dodge the responsibility
of trying to find some common thread in the various notions
which seem to have exerted the widest influence.

The dominant notions in the Hebrew inheritance appear
to be these: (1) The good is to be found in God's will — and
nowhere else; (2) knowledge of that will may be sought in
various places: history, the Torah, the synagogue or com-

munity, the Temple, or the sheer spirituality of the Chosen People. It is a standing conviction of the Old Testament that God exerts his will through natural as well as through historical and personal events; in earthquake, drought and pestilence as well as in good crops, fertility, health and other positive values. Goodness for the Hebrew meant conformity, obedience, to the will of God. Probably we ought to note the fact that the phrase " the righteous man " is much more frequently used than " the good man," which is more Greek in character, but they seem to carry essentially the same meaning after due allowance has been made for differences in the religious backgrounds of the two cultures. A righteous man is one who hears and obeys the will of God. The ethical rigor of the Hebrew idea of goodness merits our constant and considered respect. There are less coddling of man and fewer illusions about him in it than in any other tradition. Never did it let the goodness of man, or goodness as a commendable ethical ideal, get between man and God, who alone is good. Jesus was standing in the great tradition of his people when he said to the man who had addressed him as " Good Master," " Why callest thou me good? There is none good but one, even God."

The Bible gives these notions of the good and goodness by pronouncement rather than by development through careful discussion of meaning. This is one of the reasons why it was imperative for non-Jewish Christians like Justin Martyr and Clement of Alexandria to spend so much of their time " expounding the Scriptures " in regard to the meaning of righteousness. What was made obvious to the Jew by customs and expectations centuries old had to be discussed and proved to Greek and Latin minds, which had matured in a different ethico-religious climate. The idea of good as being God's will and of goodness as being obedience to that will was related to the Law, the Temple and the synagogue of the Jews as the atmosphere is to the earth. Not so in Hellenistic culture; there the conclusions had to be tested and tried all over again. That is why so much of the contemporary depreciation of "the Greek influence" as a corrupting and confusing influence on the simple, incisive truths of Hebraism is quite beside the point. If these truths had been simple to men like Augustine he would not have spent time explaining them. He gave them considerable attention precisely because their cryptic character was itself a source of confusion when they were no longer buttressed by the social and religious institutions of Judaism. It is the witness of modern missionaries that the same process must be carried on in every culture where they work. The ethical precepts of Christianity are no more self-evident to non-Christian peoples today than were those of Hebraism to the Greeks of the early centuries of our era.

Then, too, it is always in order to point out that the Greek philosophical tradition, as encountered by early Christians, had some decided views of its own on this matter of good and goodness. We need to remember that the Greek mind had been exercised about these ideas for four centuries, if not five, before the first Christian missionaries began to proclaim "the Way." No Greek thinker about whose thought we possess much information ignored or minimized them; they constitute one of the major concerns of the classical philosophical tradition of that brilliant people. It is no accident then that the great answers which ultimately emerged in Greek thought and were in final form when the Christian faith first swept over the world are the ones that Christianity leaned on most heavily after the historical process had wedded the two cultures for better or for worse into a common destiny.

Plato's conception of the good is a phase of his general philosophy, which has been outlined by Professor E. S. Brightman in this manner: "The creative factors in the universe for Plato are: God (the Demiurge or cosmic Artisan), the Pattern (the eternal ideal, corresponding to the Ideas in the earlier dialogues), and the Receptacle (the primordial chaos of space, discordant and disorderly motion). The actual world is caused by union of the forms (or Pattern) with the Receptacle. The motive of creation is the Good, the principle of value."[3]   Plato's own words from the *Timaeus* verify this analysis: "Let me tell you then why the creator made this world of generation. He was good, and the good can never have any jealousy of anything. And being free from jealousy, he desired that all things should be as like himself as they could be. This is in the truest sense the origin of creation and of the world, as we shall do well in believing on the testimony of wise men: God desired that all things should be good and nothing bad, so far as this was attainable. . . . Wherefore, using the language of probability, we may say that the world became a living creature truly endowed with soul and intelligence by the providence of God."[4]   I submit that it is a mere quibble over words to say that Plato's line of reasoning here is different in kind from that of the opening chapter of Genesis, where it is recorded that after each day's work of creation, "God saw that it was good." For both Plato and Genesis, the act of creation is to be attributed to the goodness of God. We must accept the fact that a very close parallel exists between Plato's idea that (as Dr. Brightman puts it) the good is to be regarded as God's motive in creation and the Hebrew idea that the good is God's will for creation. The difference between them is one of emphasis, so far as I can see. Plato emphasizes the good as the decisive factor in that day when God created the universe, while the Hebrew idea stresses the notion that God's will continues to be the dominant force in the created universe. Neither emphasis rules out the other; rather they work together without conflict.

Plato devotes one of his best known parables to the influence which the good exerts on the human scene. This is the parable of the cave which occurs in the opening section of the seventh book of the *Republic*.[5]   Its setting is simple and penetrating. A number of men are chained in a cave in such a way that they must face the back wall. Behind them is the entrance to the cave, through which comes what little light they get. A raised roadway runs across the mouth of the cave, and on beyond the road is a fire which furnishes the light that flickers on the wall of the cave. Whenever anything passes along the roadway its shadow is thrown on the wall as on a screen and is seen by the captives. Since that is all they see, they think it is all there is to be seen. But one day one of the captives gets free and works his way out of the cave; he discovers the fire, the objects that throw the shadows on the wall, and finally, coming entirely outside, he discovers the sun itself. Dazed by his discovery and still dazzled from looking at the sun, he hurries back to the cave to tell his comrades the truth of the whole situation. But they are suspicious of his report, and angered by his insinuation that they are not seeing properly. They require him to play one of their guessing games about the shadows on the wall. Since the gloom of the cave is all the darker for his having looked on the sun, he is easily bested by them. They " say of him that up he went and down he came without his eyes; and that it was better not even to think of ascending; and if any one tried to loose another and lead him up to the light, let them only catch the offender, and they would put him to death."

This is a tragically penetrating parable of the relationship of the good to human life and of the meaning of goodness. For goodness means the apprehension of the good and the determination henceforth to serve it alone and forswear the life of shadows. Notice how the parable closes: the man who has seen the good is under the judgment of those who have not seen it. Plato must have felt the poignant truth of this all the more when, in the later years of his life, he accepted the invitation of Dionysius the Younger, the tyrant of Sicily, to help him establish the proper government there. All went well until Plato began to suggest that Dionysius was looking at something other than the good. The tyrant didn't think so and promptly — so legend has it — threw Plato in prison, finally selling him into slavery, from which sorry state his friends redeemed him. But even before this happened to him, Plato knew that the path of goodness was essentially a venture in tragedy. Truth — the vision of the good — required the response of goodness, but power actually rested in the hands of men who had not seen the vision and were out of sympathy with anyone who had seen it and sought to tell them about it.

Aristotle's treatment of the good and goodness differs from that of Plato in several important respects. In order to appreciate it we need to see it as we saw Plato's treatment — against the backdrop of his general metaphysical system. For Aristotle, God is an essential fact in any adequate explanation of the universe. Without deity the facts of motion, growth and development are beyond explanation. Not that they become much simpler with the mere introduction of the idea of God as the Prime Mover. But this thought gave Aristotle a beginning, a point in logic behind which it was not necessary, because it would be impossible, for him to go. I do not mean to give the impression that Aristotle's God is only distantly related to events. God is the unmoved, the prime mover in whose eternal being as pure thought the entire universe has its being. Since God is pure form — i.e., without matter — his activity consists in pure thought, which is to say, thought which has thought alone for its object. He continues to influence the world not by mechanical impulse, like a push or pull, but by virtue of the perfection of his being. "God moves the world as the beloved object moves the lover," [6] is Aristotle's own poetic way of describing God's action on the world. God's nature as pure thought or perfect being makes him not only the supreme object of all knowledge but also the ultimate object of all desire.[7]

Professor Thilly gives this in summary of Aristotle's thought on God, which is basic to an understanding of his thought about the good and goodness: "The first cause is absolutely perfect, and is the highest purpose or highest good of the world. God acts on the world, not by moving it, but as a beautiful picture of an ideal acts on the soul. All beings in the world, plants, animals, men, desire the realization of their essence because of the highest good, or God; his existence is the cause of their desire. Hence God is the unifying principle of the world, the center towards which all things strive, the principle which accounts for all order, beauty, and life in the universe. God's activity consists in thought, in the contemplation of the essence of things, in the vision of beautiful forms. He is all actuality; every possibility is realized in him. He has no impressions, no sensations, no appetites, no will in the sense of desire, no feelings in the sense of passions; he is pure intelligence. Our intellect is discursive, our knowledge is piecemeal, moving along step by step; God's thinking is intuitive: he sees all things at once and sees them whole. He is free from pain and passion, and is supremely happy." [8]

A careful comparison of Plato and Aristotle on the relationship between God and the good suggests one difference which seems to be important. Plato makes good the motive of God in creation; Aristotle would apply the attribute to God only in so far as He is the object of man's rational desire. For Plato, good is an intrinsic fact about God; for Aristotle, good is an intrinsic fact about man's response to God. This difference suggests that the cosmic status of the good is more objectively stated by Plato than by Aristotle. While God is certainly no less real to Aristotle than to Plato, it appears that his (God's) goodness is dependent upon his being the object of rational contemplation. Naturally, the supreme goodness for man is the uninterrupted rational enjoyment of God. By virtue of the faculty of reason, which is the distinctive attribute of man, some measure of goodness is always open to man; the greatest measure of course to the philosopher, who best understands God's ways of being and acting. "In the contemplation of the first principles of knowledge and being man participates in that activity of pure thought which constitutes the eternal perfection of the divine nature." [9] Therefore the highest good for man is found in theoretical inquiry and contemplation of truth, rather than in practical activity.

Another way to put the matter is this: The good for any item in existence is self-fulfillment, the attainment of its predetermined end. For man, whose highest faculty is reason, the highest good is the fulfillment of the capacity which he shares with deity of being able to think about thought or pure forms.

Still another influential figure in the Greek tradition must be consulted on the meaning of the good and goodness before we are prepared to study the ways in which these various ideas influenced Christian thought. Plotinus, the greatest Neo-Platonist, introduces an attitude toward the use of the concept good as applied to God that has haunted subsequent Christian thought on ethics and morals. Dean Inge is well within the truth when he writes, " The importance of Plotinus in the history of thought can hardly be exaggerated." [10] God, for Plotinus, is the ineffable, the unknowable One in whose reality consists the absolute unity of the universe. No attribute can be applied to God without limiting him in some nonpermissible manner. Consequently Plotinus does not follow Plato's attribution of the good to God. He is more in sympathy with the Aristotelian meaning of goodness as man's proper rational response to God, though he would never say with Aristotle that man can describe the reality of God. True knowledge, for Plotinus, is the state wherein one steps beyond the domain of rational concepts and contemplates God in a state of mystical ecstasy and conceptual-less enjoyment. Such knowledge cannot be had for the asking or brought into being by any known formula. As Dean Inge remarks, " it is part of the fundamental sanity of Plotinus that he always speaks of the vision of the One as an exceedingly rare experience. It is the consummation of a life-long quest of the highest, to be earned only by intense contemplation and unceasing self-discipline." [11]

To return for a moment to Plotinus' thought about God, his favorite ways of referring to God are as the " There," the one " Center," the " All," the " Absolute," the " Source," the " It," or the " One." The nearest he ever comes to an ascription of goodness to God is this exhortation: "Therefore, let each become godlike and beautiful who cares to see God and Beauty: the Primal Good and the Primal Beauty have one dwelling-place, and thus, always, Beauty's seat is There." [12] But even in this passage it is apparent that the "dwelling-place" and the "There" are ultimate, rather than the concepts of good and beauty. Let no one think that Plotinus depreciates beauty and goodness. The truth is that few philosophers have exalted them quite as much as he; many of his paragraphs read like hymns in praise of beauty and the good. Yet the careful reader will always be conscious of the fact that, however excellent these and other concepts are in the lower reaches of the world, they simply are not to be applied to God in his essence. Plotinus' own words on this matter leave no room for doubt: "It is in truth unspeakable; for if you say anything of It, you make It a particular thing. Now That which transcends all things, even the most august Divine Mind, cannot be regarded as one of them; nor can we give It a name or predicate aught of It. . . . We speak indeed about It, but Itself we do not express; nor have we knowledge or intellection of It. But though It escapes our knowledge, It does not entirely escape us; for we can say what It is not, if not what It is." [13]

This emphasis of Plotinus exerted a mighty influence in Christian thought through the writings of Augustine and Dionysius the Areopagite. And, as every good Barthian who revels in his master's description of God as "the wholly Other" knows, the influence of this whole Plotinian tradition of ultimate irrationality is still with us. Christian mystics have made abundant use of it, as you might well expect. But for our present purpose no extensive criticism of Plotinus' thought is in order. We leave it with the simple notation of the fact that it does not equate God and Good. It regards the good as one of the primal categories through which God expresses himself in the lower reaches of the world; it regards goodness as meaning devotion to God and the continual search for, first, an understanding of him, and second, the experience of union with him.

Augustine does more borrowing than thinking in his description of the meaning of good and goodness. But he borrows from good men, principally Plato as interpreted by Plotinus, and the apostle Paul. Obviously we shall not want to attempt anything like a careful outlining of Augustine's thought, which by any method of reckoning is one of the most fertile in Christian history. Not the least reason for its fecundity is the fact that Augustine was in turn a skeptic, a Manichaean, a skeptic again, a Neo-Platonist, a believer in the Scriptures, and finally a convert to the faith. He could have said what Tennyson was later to say: "I am a part of all that I have met," for in truth each of these intellectual experiences left its mark either in his method of thought or in the conclusions wherein his mind seemed finally to come to rest. So far as the good is concerned, he seized on the notion common to Hebraism and Platonism that good is tied in tightly with the concept of God. His reasoning and feeling, as summarized by Dr. A. C. McGiffert, run like this: "As God is the only real being, he is the only real good. Apart from him there is no reality and hence apart from him there is no good. Man's highest good is to depend upon God and cleave to him. It is the language of philosophy as well as of piety when Augustine says: ' God, to turn away from whom is to fall; to turn back to whom is to rise again; to abide in whom is to stand fast. God, to depart from whom is to die; to return to whom is to come to life again; to dwell in whom is to live.' " [14]

Like so many resounding conclusions, this one literally proved to be little more than an introduction to Augustine's most aggravating metaphysical problem, i.e., the existence of evil. Like Paul and all other serious Christian thinkers, the good bishop of Hippo found that it is most difficult to affirm the reality of good without affirming the reality of evil. Yet to do this puts the brakes on any easy identification of God and the good, unless of course you desire to deal with a cosmic devil as the incarnation of evil. It was precisely this dualism in Manichaeism that drove Augustine to Neo-Platonism, which denied the reality of evil, saying that it is merely the "absence of good," a kind of vacuum in a good cosmos. Augustine the Christian was not too satisfied with the Neo-Platonic solution, since he keeps coming back to it for a fresh try at proof, but it is the best one he can get his intellectual hands on. His famous adaptation of it is that "evil is the shadow of good." Good does not require evil in order to be real, but evil does require good in order to be real. Good is positive, is the presence of that which is positive; it is the object of reliable knowledge and will. Evil is the absence of these, metaphysically speaking.

Augustine does not really leave the matter there; his devotion to Paul would not let him. Under the propulsion of Paul's writings, in which evil, sin and their infernal ilk are terribly real, Augustine is finally forced to accept the position that the corrupt or evil will is but the manifestation of a depraved or fallen human nature, and as such is at least real enough in God's sight to require the incarnation of himself in Christ in order properly to deal with it. Brooding over the problem of why God should be so concerned brought Augustine to his celebrated emphasis upon the love and the grace of God. Whatever God does is rooted and grounded in love. The only truly appropriate response to him is that of complete faith springing from an unquestioning love of him. So to love God is no fatalistic cry of "Kismet"; it is to rest confident in his government of the world and history, for the impulse of his love moves through these. When Augustine writes in this mood, the good and God are synonymous terms. And — still in this mood — goodness means the absolute love of God, absolute commitment to his holy will. But when he writes in the Pauline mood in which God is locked in eternal yet deadly conflict with "the powers and principalities" not alone of the earth but also of other worlds, the good and goodness take on a somewhat different hue. God becomes the champion of the good, which is his will for the world, and goodness means the service of him in this never ending conflict which begins within one's own soul and extends to the threshold of heaven itself.   Platonism and Neo-Platonism dominate, if they do not determine, Augustine in the first of these moods, even as Hebraism and Manichaeism do in the second.   In both moods the good is real, and goodness is a definite way of life in the service of the good.   Augustine everywhere echoes the prophetic insistence that goodness consists in obedience to God, though he would add that this obedience is made possible by the grace of God in Christ.

Thomas Aquinas recurs repeatedly to the problem of the good and goodness in his voluminous writings.   His thought here as elsewhere borrows its logical form and metaphysical principles from Aristotle while keeping true to the essential content of the Christian religion.   It is unfair to say, as is frequently said, that Thomas merely baptized Aristotle.   It seems to me that he used Aristotle in quite an objective manner as the philosopher whose system of thought was best fitted to bring out in indisputable form the essential truth of the Christian faith.   The use he makes of Aristotle's thought on the good and goodness is a case in point.   It is well to remember that before Thomas knew Aristotle's works he was well versed in the orthodox theological tradition of the church, which is to say that he was familiar with the general modes of thought, and the conclusions to which they led, of Platonism, Neo-Platonism, and the various modifications of them that had grown up in the church's schools.   He discovered in Aristotle what these other systems lacked: logical rigor.   Consequently he recast orthodox Christian thought in Aristotelian terms.   For him, " God . . . is the first and final (purposive) cause of the universe.   He is pure actuality or energy; if he were mere potential being, something else would be required to make him actual or real, and he would not be the first cause.   As pure actuality, God is absolutely simple and absolutely perfect; he is also absolute intelligence, absolute con-

sciousness, and absolute will." [15] Moving from this metaphysical background, Thomas reaches a clear and decisive
statement of the relationship between God and the good. He
affirms that "God made everything for a purpose — for the
purpose of revealing his goodness in creation —, that the nature of everything points in the direction of this purpose, and
that every creature will realize the divine idea and reveal the
goodness of God by realizing its true being. The highest
good, therefore, objectively considered, is God; subjectively
viewed, that is, for creatures, it is their greatest possible perfection, or likeness to God." [16]

This short summary of Thomas' thought provides us with
the essential information we need. Goodness, for God, is the
contemplation of his perfection; goodness, for man, is a state
of blessedness in which he realizes both his true self and its
kinship with God. Empirically, goodness, for man, consists
in curbing sinful desires and overcoming various temptations
to worship something other than God. In this struggle the
aid of the church is invaluable since by the sacraments she is
able to impart wisdom, courage and strength. When doubts
lift their head the church, by recourse to the revealed truth
incarnate in her dogma, imparts unshakable assurance and a
peace that passeth all understanding. Whoever desires to attain the state of blessedness — which, for Thomas, is a child of
the union of the Hebrew concept of "righteousness" and the
Greek concept of "goodness" — will not fail to make full use
of such assistance.

Thus it will be seen both how like Aristotle's thought and
how different from it is that of the great Dominican thinker.
He reaffirms what we have seen to be the strongest tradition
in Christian thought on the matter of the good: God and the
good are inseparable. However much mystics may object to
applying any attribute to deity, we may rest assured that this
one will stand: "The Lord is good; his mercy endureth
forever."

As we think our way back over what we have discovered

in the thought of these pivotal figures in our intellectual heritage, several important points stand out as having occurred in some form in all of them. A brief restatement of these points may be useful:

1.   God and the good are vitally related. They may be inseparable — at least the Hebrews, Plato, Augustine (in one of his moods) and Thomas Aquinas thought so and made the conviction central in their thought.

2.   Goodness consists in man's proper approach to God. " Proper " is the word to watch in this statement. For Plato and Aristotle a " proper" approach was largely an affair of intellectual apprehension of God. For the Hebrews it meant implicit obedience to the will of God, which was thought to reside in the Torah, in the Temple, in the history of the Chosen People, or in the ethical issues of any given day. For Plotinus, " proper " could mean only an earnest effort to transcend all known categories of thought and experience and be lost in an ineffable union with the One. For Augustine and Aquinas, it meant obedience to and oneness with God.

3.   Goodness is a two-way road; he who travels it both gives to and receives from God. If a man dedicates his mind to the apprehension of the Eternal Ideas (Plato), or the Eternal Forms (Aristotle), or the One (Plotinus), or the Creator and Redeemer of the World (Augustine, Aquinas), he will actually be strengthened by what he discovers. There is food for him to eat along the way; he has meat to eat that others know not of. There is no self-pity among these men as they contemplate the price one must pay for goodness. It is worth all they can pay and more too. Their only concern seems to be that when they have paid their all it will still not be enough. Paul's well worn words of comfort are in point: " I can do all things through Christ who strengtheneth me." This undergirding of reverence and trust will be found in all serious thought about the relationship between the good and goodness.

The implications of all this for the Christian faith, and for

us who must preach it, are too obvious to need extensive statement, but it has been my experience that one more summary
of such matters is seldom amiss!

1.   The first implication is that this is a moral universe.
It is indeed a tribute to the pervasive character of our intellectual tradition that we repeat these words almost glibly,
with all too little appreciation of either the fight they had for
their life or the tremendous gulf which yawns between them
and their opposite: this is *not* a moral universe.   Take two
blank sheets of paper and write one of these assertions at the
top of each; then fill in each page with the indisputable implications of the heading.   It will be an enlightening and hum-
bling exercise, I assure you.   The page headed "This is a
moral universe" is fairly likely to be filled with the stuff
which goes into our noble resolutions and excellent inten-
tions, while the other page will contain the stuff which gets
into our actions.   The former page will tell the story of what
we might be; the latter, of what we are.   Of course the revealing fact about such a simple exercise as this is that it
reminds us of the tragic glory of the human enterprise: we
can choose to ignore the moral character of the universe, but
we cannot escape its meaning.   Something of this may have
been in Emerson's mind as he wrote:

> "They reckon ill who leave me out;
>   When me they fly, I am the wings;
>   I am the doubter and the doubt,
>   And I the hymn the Brahmin sings." [17]

The cryptic lines from the prophet, "The soul that sinneth,
it shall die," and Paul's discovery, "The wages of sin is death,"
point up the same general fact; namely, that we live in a
world which is not morally neutral.   It is good at heart and in
basic action, but its goodness has not made robots of human
beings, requiring that we be good; it has, in the words of an
ancient myth, set before us the tree of life and the tree of
death and bidden us choose.   And choose each person and

people must. So runs the meaning of the assertion that this is a moral universe.

2.   A second implication of the time-tested relationship between God and goodness is that God's good will is manifest in the creation and the redemption of the world. While the Greek thinkers would accept the word " creation," I feel sure they would demur against the word "redemption," which is essentially a Christian contribution to theology. But the important thing suggested by this latter term is that God is no absentee landlord, no deistic deity, no inhabitant of heavens so far removed from earth as not to know what is going on here and, what is worse, not to care. The Christian conception of God is radically different. As one Oriental put it to a missionary, " You have a strange God. He gets you into trouble and gets you out again. I want to know more about him." As we look at the long bloody confusion of human history, never plainer than now, we are tempted to lose heart in human nature and cancel out our faith in the reality of a good God. But the plain fact is that we can be " more than conquerors " even of the infamy of history if one of the sources of our strength is the belief in the reality of a good God who is not only Creator but also Redeemer of the world. From the vision of him which we catch in Jesus Christ we know beyond all reasonable doubt that his love for the world is of such quality that it both must be served with a whole heart and will finally emerge triumphant in its struggle to redeem the world.

3.   The only proper reaction of man to God is that of complete commitment to God's good will.   There finally comes a time and place where halfway measures and halting steps are worse than no measures or steps at all. Augustine discovered this when he found himself praying, in effect, " O God, give me chastity, but not yet! " Usually, being human, we dodge the recognition of the necessity of commitment as long as our little houses give us reasonable shelter from calamitous events. But life has a way of catching up with us. It caught up with Paul and reduced him to crying, "Who

shall deliver me from this living death? " It caught up with the famous English preacher, Robertson of Brighton, who saw one certainty after another wither before the onslaught of nineteenth-century skepticism until he finally reached, as his last stand, the conviction, " It's right to do right." I am of the opinion that it catches up with us all, not just once but repeatedly, largely because we become careless about our relationship with God, permitting it to become professional, not keeping it keen, sensitive, strong, humble. Commitment to God means something more than a sense of being *en rapport* with God in a personal way; it means a constantly deepening and widening concern for the growth of righteousness and goodness in life. Consequently the achievement of goodness involves insight, sacrifice and courage of the highest order. The Christian faith knows no short cuts to salvation, but it does know of a " strength sufficient for every trial."

REFERENCES

[1] A. A. Milne, *Four Plays* (New York: G. P. Putnam's Sons, 1932), p. 27.

[2] H. O. Taylor, *The Medieval Mind*, 2 vols. (New York: The Macmillan Co., 1911), II, 433.

[3] E. S. Brightman, *A Philosophy of Religion* (New York: Prentice-Hall, Inc., 1940), p. 339.

[4] *The Dialogues of Plato*, translated into English by B. Jowett, M.A. 2 vols. (New York: Random House, 1937), II, 13–14.

[5] *Ibid.*, I, 773 ff.

[6] Quoted by Durant, *The Story of Philosophy*, p. 81.

[7] *Dictionary of Philosophy*, p. 82 *passim.*

[8] Thilly, *History of Philosophy*, p. 85.

[9] *Dictionary of Philosophy*, p. 22.

[10] *Encyclopedia Britannica*, 14th ed., XVIII, 81.

[11] *Ibid.*, XVIII, 82.

[12] *Enneads*, I, vi. 9. In Turnbull, *The Essence of Plotinus*, p. 50.

[13] *Enneads*, v. iii. *passim.* In Turnbull, *Tongues of Fire*, p. 328.

[14] McGiffert, *History of Christian Thought*, II, 86.

[15] Thilly, *op. cit.*, p. 196.

[16] *Ibid.*, p. 198.

[17] Emerson, " Brahma."

For God so loved the world, that he gave his only begotten Son, that whosoever believeth in him should not perish, but have everlasting life.

John 3:16

And now abideth faith, hope, love, these three; but the greatest of these is love.

I Corinthians 13:13

Beloved, let us love one another: for love is God; and everyone that loveth is born of God, and knoweth God.

I John 4:7

God is love; and he that dwelleth in love dwelleth in God, and God in him.

I John 4:16

. V .

The Reality of Love

WE HAVE been studying the various ways in which the philosophical heritage of the Christian faith has taken form. We began with a momentous event in early Christian history — the scattering of the small sect of Palestinian Christians throughout the rest of the Greco-Roman world. For a variety of reasons, not the least of which was recurring persecution in Jerusalem, they sought out new homes in other, more hospitable places. Not all left, of course, and so long as those "who had known Jesus" remained alive in Jerusalem they were the acknowledged pillars of the growing church. But with their death the center of gravity for the entire group shifted westward with great rapidity.

It was then that the simple, straightforward faith of those who accepted Jesus as the messiah came to grips with the long philosophical tradition of ancient Greece. This tradition was firmly established, albeit in a corrupted form, in many schools throughout the eastern half of the Mediterranean area, especially in Alexandria. Immediately the process of fusion got under way and carried on through succeeding centuries, until today it is simply impossible to separate the strands and have anything approximating the Christian tradition left. We saw how the crucial thinking about the great values truth, beauty and goodness had been done, partly by the Hebrews to be sure, but with the intellectual skeleton coming from the Greeks. We saw also how the continuing philosophical tradition (which no more stopped with Aristotle than Christian thought stopped with Paul) acted as guide, check and spur to Christian theology in periods of confusion in later centuries. However much theological purists may choose to kick against the prick of fact, the basic fact still stands: the intellectual framework of the Christian faith is a philosophical tradition which rests principally upon the thought of the great Greeks Plato and Aristotle.

Our problem today is to determine the relationship between the basic philosophical tradition of Christianity and the oft-used concept of love. Let me, in a sentence, suggest the conclusion toward which the facts will lead us: The affirmation of the importance of love as a cosmic principle and as the strongest fact in social life was never clearly seen before the Christian religion had thought its way into a vital relationship with both Judaism and Greek philosophy.

The Hebrews had come close to the notion of love in their thought on righteousness, mercy and forgiveness. This is especially true of the book of Hosea and of the prophecies now lumped together and attributed to the Second Isaiah. But even these seers seem never to have used the word love to signify anything beyond the bounds of (1) social relationships within their own race and (2) the proper attitude of man to God. You will look in vain for " love " as a basic description of God's concern for man — and it is precisely this emphasis which makes the Christian use of the concept so distinctive. Even when, in the Old Testament writings, the concept of love is used in these two ways that come closest to its Christian use, it is treated in an almost offhand manner, as being synonymous with mercy, or forgiveness, or righteousness. The clearest proof we could ask for on this fact is, I believe, the consensus among contemporary Jewish scholars that the Christian doctrine of love cannot be found except in rudimentary form in their tradition. Not that they regret this. For them, generally, love is to be subordinated to justice as the fundamental religious value.

The dominant philosophical tradition of Greece came close to the notion of love as a metaphysical principle, both in its general emphasis upon the values of truth, beauty and goodness and in one specific book of Plato, the *Symposium*. In this writing Plato is investigating the meaning of love. He goes behind the usually accepted meaning of it as being the affection-bond between human beings; nor is he satisfied to stop the search with a consideration of love as the bond between man and woman by which procreation becomes possible. He pushes the inquiry one step further and speculates about love as the basic life-principle in all created things in the universe. Now if Plato had done more than suggest this last step he would have unearthed much, if not most, of what the Christian religion at a much later date was going to mean by the concept as a philosophical principle. But Plato made nothing more of it so far as his writings are concerned. It does not emerge in other dialogues. In the *Republic*, as in the *Laws*, the fundamental value or virtue is either justice or wisdom, but not love. So we must conclude that Plato either did not see the possibility of love as the fundamental value or, having seen it, rejected it. If the latter was the case he did no more than a good many later philosophers have done who have been exposed, shall we say, to the Christian tradition all their lives.

But a further fact remains to be noted about Plato's dialogues. Brooding over those immortal discussions of justice, knowledge, truth and the good is the haunting recognition that these values are both essential to human life and *essential to each other* if they are to make their greatest contribution to life. Plato's vigorous mind could not rest with a superb discussion of any one of them. They all pressed in for consideration when he tried to single out one. They emerge, in dialogue after dialogue, not singly but collectively, though specific dialogues set out to consider them separately. One crucial fact about the nature of these values is the way they clamor collectively for recognition in every major Platonic dialogue. There is a sense of incompleteness in each discussion which permits some one value to occupy the stage of attention — and no one is more keenly aware of that incompleteness than Plato himself. Always he seems almost ready to close his hands on the fact that if you want to get at the truth of any one value you must consider the value-structure of the world in which it occurs. Or, to put it another way, if you do not want to consider values *collectively* you cannot consider them *separately* with any degree of conclusiveness. We shall shortly see how much can and must be made of this cohesive character of values.

It is too easy to say that the Greeks did not have a word for this fact; it is doubtful that they were ever keenly aware of it as a fact. Certainly they never tried to nail it down in clear-cut terms as a specific problem to be thought about. Perhaps their intense individualism prevented them from doing full justice to the possibility that this cohesive tendency within values is an ultimate fact in reality. It is very significant that when Plato is describing the vision supreme, vouchsafed only to philosophers, it is as a sea of beautiful ideas or forms, not as the principle of Idea or Form; i.e., they are separate entities. But, for whatever reason, the Greek thinkers did not deal with any reality or idea which might reasonably be likened to the Christian idea of love. They talked much about ultimate values (pluralized) but did not include love among them.

The most creative new fact which the Christian faith brought to its marriage with Greek thought was the conviction of the reality of love as a fundamental principle for interpreting life and the universe. You may object that our New Testament nowhere contains any careful discussion of love in that sense. And your objection is well taken, but not therefore decisive. If the New Testament does little more than suggest the pre-eminence of love, the proper explanation lies in the then prevalent notion that history was standing on the brink of a fearful final reckoning, in which philosophical clarity would admittedly be of slight avail. But as time moved on and the dread day (or the blessed day, depending upon your attitude) failed to dawn, the leading Christian minds began a careful evaluation of their heritage — Jewish, Greek, and the deposit of early Christian lore and fact. The moment they began to do this the cryptic affirmations of the New Testament became open doors leading to a new appreciation of the reality of love as a cosmic fact, and hence as a principle of interpretation in explaining events. This early discovery of the profound depths in the idea and principle of love I take to be one of the truly momentous moments in the development of Christian thought. But having paid tribute to the importance of this discovery I must add that, for reasons to which we shall presently turn, it has been impossible to do full justice to love as a philosophical principle until the last one hundred years or less.

I do not mean to minimize the fact that, from the beginning, the Christians sensed the basic character of love in their fellowship and in their relationship to God through Christ. That assuredly is one of the reasons why men came to the Christian group from the folds of the many philosophical schools and movements that were more purely Greek in lineage. Clement of Alexandria was one of these persons. He left no doubt that, in his judgment, he had entered into a wholly new way of life. I suppose no word of his is better known than his description of what he found in Christ: " He turned our sunsets into sunrises." Certain as Clement was of the very great benefit of knowledge in the achievement of Christian virtue, he never failed to add that truly beneficial knowledge must be rooted in the sincere love of God. Those well worn and always enriching words of the Gospel of John assure us that the early Christians saw the reality of love: " For God so loved the world, that he gave his only begotten son, that whosoever believeth in him should not perish, but have everlasting life." No man could write that, nor would it have been treasured as priceless through the ages, without some discernment of the ultimate meaning of love. The same can be said for that sobering passage in I John which describes the token of Christian discipleship: "By this shall all men know that ye are my disciples, that ye bear love one to another." Several hundred years later the troubled spirit of Augustine finally found peace through the full acceptance of the Christian faith. It is instructive to note how he fondles the words "light," "peace" and "love" in his account of how he felt when the decision was made. Nor did he ever forget to honor God's power as love as well as his power as grace in making his conversion possible.

The point I hope to make by citing such instances from the history of the early centuries is that they clearly show that those who came into Christian fellowship were, as a rule, acutely aware of the fact of its difference from any other kind of association, and their minds could not rest until they had tried to explain it. Such explanations usually center in the word love, meaning not so much their proper response to God as God's essential concern for man made manifest in the Christian fellowship.

You can count on it that Thomas Aquinas does voluminous justice to the meaning of love! He sees at once that it is a fundamental matter. After a searching study of Aristotle's definition of cause and his description of the various kinds of causes, Thomas adds the characteristic and revolutionary Christian touch: "Love is the deepest spring of all." But Aquinas, like Augustine, for all his remarkable penetration into the fundamentals of Christian thought and life did not have at hand anything like the amount of evidence which we now possess for saying, "God is love." I am of the opinion that one of the reasons why so much of the thought of these two great souls seemed to lead them into a denial of the worth of the world was that the more clearly they saw into the depths of the fact of love, the more out of harmony it was with what they knew about the world's fundamental nature. Their knowledge of the meaning of love was much ahead of their knowledge of the structure and meaning of the world. Living as they did in an age which knew little

science and had wrapped what little it did know in the suf-
focating blankets of superstition, astrology and magic, or else
in a blighting mechanism like Lucretius', they could scarcely
reach any other conclusion than that a fundamental antago-
nism exists between God as love and the world as it is.

A basic philosophical and metaphysical view of reality
congenial to the full development of the meaning of love was,
as I have said, not possible until less than a hundred years
ago. Lest you think this statement an uncritical worship of
modernity at the expense of antiquity, consider these facts.
It was not until after Darwin, whose great work on evolution
was published in the latter half of the nineteenth century,
that it became actually impossible for a thoughtful person to
subscribe to a mechanistic and deistic view of reality. It
would be unfair to credit Darwin with having alone wrought
this near-miracle. He has been singled out because of what
was happening not alone through him but also all around him.
Scientific advances in various fields placed new knowledge
about the universe at the disposal of the philosophers. The
new physics shook off the mechanism of the eighteenth and
nineteenth centuries. True enough, it soon wound up wres-
tling with the facts underlying the principles of uncertainty
and relativity, and these hold serious problems for the philosopher, but they are quite different from the ones that had
previously taxed his mind. At least we are now living in the
world about which William James used to dream — " a wide-
open universe." You will have to admit its wide-openness
when you realize that it is a world in which a straight line is
no longer the shortest distance between two points, in which
parallel lines will meet if extended indefinitely, in which — or
so the mathematicians say — two plus two no longer equals
four! Other sciences joined physics in shaking the old world
view to its very foundation. Psychology began to explore
the nature of the self, especially the self as manifested in
mind or consciousness. Sociology began to gather facts on
the nature of society — not only the more culturally advanced

societies but the primitive ones as well. Social psychology
wove the two together and launched a most fruitful research
into the meaning of self in society. So, all in all, the last one
hundred years have seen more concentrated, purposive and
fruitful scientific research than all the rest of recorded history put together.

We probably ought to underscore the further fact about
this last century that world events produced a calamitous
climate of opinion in which it was not only possible but also
highly advisable to think new thoughts about the meaning
of life, history and human destiny. The unity of the entire
human enterprise, for good or evil, was becoming increasingly apparent, though reactionaries in business, politics and
religion tried to face backward even as they were being swept
forward by the floodtide of events. Then, too, a popular
awareness of something deeply out of joint was abroad.
There were too many and too frequent depressions; there was
too much and too terrible insecurity; there were too many
searching questions and too few creative answers — and a
great fear slowly settled on the spirit of man, the same fear
that, Canon Charles Raven says, haunted the world into which
Christianity came in the first century, " the fear that man is
about played out." Certain brute facts remain to be noted:
the unparalleled growth of population, the necessity of access
on the part of all peoples to the goods essential to life, the
development of communication and transportation — all of
which forced upon civilization a certain kind of unity, and
carried within themselves unimagined potentialities for
greater unity or more tragic disunity than had ever before
been experienced.

The philosophical systems of our time have begun to mir-
ror certain new facts in addition to old ones that have been
able to hold their place. One such new fact is that of unpre-
dictable change within the larger areas of predictable behavior. The physicist discovered that he could not tell what
any given atom was going to do, but could compute statistical

averages about the action of a " stream of atoms " that were
wholly reliable.   The biologist was confronted by similar
phenomena.   He could predict confidently that most of the
offspring of an animal would be normal, but could not say
that any given one would be (i.e., prior to its actual birth).
Whether the insurance companies got their policy of gam-
bling on the statistical table rather than on the individual
from these facts, I do not know!   Such scientific discoveries
led to the formulation of the principle of uncertainty as applied to the exact sciences, and the principle of contingency
as applied to the life-studies.   It is not to be said that these
principles supplanted the older one of certainty and orderliness, but it is to be said that they supplemented them.
Philosophical minds brooding over these facts and theories developed the principle of discontinuity and recognized that henceforth that principle must be accepted as of
fundamental value in any adequate interpretation of reality
as known.

A second new fact with which philosophy began to wrestle is this: Any unit is always an aspect or phase of a larger
whole from which it is actually, though not abstractly, inseparable.   This is true of the atom, or electron, or proton, or
any other unit in physics.   The unit is never found alone; it
is always in combination.   This same principle applies to the
human self, the social psychologists discovered.   There is no
longer any use exercising ourselves over the question of what
would happen to a baby left to grow up alone on a desert is-
land.   The answer is simple: he wouldn't grow up at all, he
would die.   It is hard to describe our vital interdependence
in a more forceful way than that.

New facts like these have created a tremendous stir in
philosophy.   Gone is the day when the professor could lecture comfortably from the same set of notes year after year!
It is not at all unlikely that the weekly journal of science or
philosophy will carry an announcement which challenges
some fundamental principle or other.   When Michelson, the

famous physicist, first heard of Einstein's theory of relativity he said, " I hope it isn't true, because if it is we shall have to rethink the whole of physical theory.   But if it is true we shall have to do it! "   As you would expect, when such new facts upset the old mechanistic theories of reality, a multitude of philosophical problems came tumbling out for re-examination, many of them crucial problems in ethical theory — free will, obligation and value, to name only three of the most pressing ones.

The total result has been — and continues to be — one of the most chaotic periods in the whole history of philosophy. " Where nothing is forbidden everything is permitted " comes all too close to being an apt description of the frantic way in which philosophy set herself to explore any and every possible theoretical explanation.

But there are signs that it is a creative chaos, which is to say that it is slowly beginning to take some sort of orderly form.   About twelve years ago Professor Arthur Murphy wrote that, in his judgment, the outlines of a genuinely new philosophy were beginning to stir the waters of modern thought.   He believed this emerging philosophy to be the joint result of the creative work of John Dewey and A. N. Whitehead.   A multitude of creative thinkers has come to the fore in every field of philosophic inquiry: Jeans, Eddington, Compton, George Herbert Mead, C. I. Lewis, E. S. Ames, Croce, Unamuno, Nicolai Hartmann, Brightman, Wieman, Hartshorne.   This list could be extended to much greater lengths, but more important than the length of the list is recognition of the very important fact that several systematic thinkers have tried to think the whole flux into a system, " to see life steadily and to see it whole."   S. Alexander in *Space, Time and Deity* makes a truly tremendous effort to piece together a unified view of the universe.   We have repeatedly mentioned the work of Henri Bergson, A. N. Whitehead and John Dewey and merely refer to them again because of their stature among the contemporary thinkers who have not been cowed into panic or cynical despair by the unruly nature of the world as known.

The most important thing about all these systems is that they are reactions to the new facts and theories about the fundamental nature of life and the universe. Undoubtedly we are living too close to them and the period they seek to interpret to evaluate properly their permanent worth, but by sighting over them we can determine the way in which modern thought is tending. These new directions are so different from the old ones that Archbishop Temple, in his Gifford lectures entitled *Nature, Man and God,* offers the opinion that the period of philosophy which began with Descartes is coming to an end and a new one is beginning. To my mind, the most illuminating thing about these new movements in philosophic thought is the way in which reflections upon the nature of the universe, of life and of human value are beginning to be seen as giving body, as it were, to the Christian affirmation that "God is love." Professor Charles Hartshorne, writing in the preface to his *Man's Vision of God,* says: "The ground for this book is the conviction that a magnificent intellectual content — far surpassing that of such systems as Thomism, Spinozism, German idealism, positivism (old and new) — is implicit in the religious faith most briefly expressed in the three words, God is love." [1] He then goes on to turn in a splendid appraisal of the logical problems which must be met (and he meets them!) in clarifying the meaning of God. It would be difficult to find more direct evidence of the fact that philosophy is now in a position to investigate the proposition that love is the ultimate principle of philosophic interpretation. Philosophy of religion cannot be expected to continue to bring in, as being satisfactory, the same old theories about God, man and the good life, unless these have been tested against the emerging interpretation of new facts. It is frequently the case that major alterations are not necessary; but in almost every case the form of the ideas must be recast in terms of what we now have reason to believe is true about the world in which we live. It is hard to see how we can object to such modifications unless we are ready to repudiate our honorable faith in the proposition, "Ye shall know the truth and the truth shall make you free."

We get a fair sample of how this process of redefinition is working when we seek a careful statement of the relationship which appears to obtain between the idea of God and the factual knowledge we have about the nature of the world. When we say, "God is love," we have not so much stated a conclusion as laid out an area for investigation. The fuller and (rationally though not emotionally) more definitive statement of what this means will run, in my judgment, something like this: *God or love is the principle of integration operative in the universe which is most clearly seen on the human level in the growth of values.* I repeat, such a definition must be regarded as indicating areas of fact in which we shall find reality behaving, as it were, in a very definite manner. The definition will be found, upon reflection, to point to two sorts of fact: (1) the structure and behavior of the world as known through science; (2) the world whose nature we encounter in everyday experiences of values such as friendship, love, responsibility, obligation and loyalty.

Let me say with utmost emphasis that this twofold designation is not intended to convey a distinction between fact and value, as though they inhabited different worlds of reality. That seems to me to be positively not true. Values are facts, and every fact is undoubtedly an integral part of some larger structure of fact which is a value. Nothing but damage will be done by continuing the distinction between fact and value as it was drawn by German theologians under the Kantian influence about a hundred years ago. The distinction was drawn as a way of rescuing religion from the mechanistic view of the universe which was prevalent at that time, but it saved religion by the dubious process of sterilizing it, by declaring its irrelevance to the world of fact. Now that the mechanistic world is gone, put to death by the scientists themselves, and now that we can recognize the very great damage done by the distinction, let us beware of drawing it again. It is and always will be as pernicious as it is false. A friendship is as truly a fact as an atom. The reason for accepting the twofold way of acquiring our information about reality is that to the best of our knowledge we can experience a friendship but cannot experience an atom. It takes all the calculating cunning of an Arthur Compton even to get a picture of where atoms have been; so we ordinary mortals will have to take his word for their existence. Some facts are simpler than others; some facts, like that of death, are enormously complicated when viewed in their true perspective.

The definition given earlier points further to the problem of method in getting facts about reality, and indicates that the method of observation and reason, variously refined to fit the types of material under observation, must be regarded as adequate. What I am now saying amounts to this: Philosophy can recognize no truth as *philosophic truth* which comes from some special medium of knowledge like that claimed by revelation. As I understand the spirit of philosophy in this matter it simply does not concern itself with the knowledge-claim of such deliverances. They come like bolts out of the blue and refuse to permit anyone to examine their credentials; so it is no wonder that any philosopher determined to test the validity of a conclusion by careful examination of the method of thought whereby it was reached finds no place for the so-called revealed truths in his system. Before you who are heated advocates of revelation as a valid way of knowledge pass judgment upon the philosopher who reacts in this fashion, please remember that so eminent a philosopher and theologian as Thomas Aquinas took precisely that attitude. There are two ways of reaching truth, he said — one that of revelation which gives us the dogmas of the faith and which is the especial charge of the church; the other that of reason which must deal rationally (i.e., fact by fact) with reality as encountered through sense perception. The latter sort of truth is rational truth, and cannot be expected to validate revealed truth; neither of course should it contradict it since by definition all truth is one and revelation is infallible. I cite this distinction to point out that even theologians admit the utter impossibility of merging into one body of interpretation truths delivered by revelation and truths garnered from facts.

It is my own opinion that the fundamental positions of the Christian faith do not need the validation of any such esoteric form of knowledge as that which usually masquerades under the name of revelation. Of this I am sure: Anyone who falls back on revelations, whether from the Bible or the church or the Inner Light, should be prepared to proceed with the greatest care in the use of the method. Above all he should not seek to merge such deliverances with the hard-won truths of experience. Nor should he blame the person who, believing with the Cambridge Platonists, though for different reasons, that " to follow reason is to follow God," insists that he is not going to admit such deliverances into the fold of truth until and unless they can pass the tests of truth. We have learned too much from such men in these latter days to dismiss them as secularists or skeptics. One of the merits of the definition presented above is that it proposes to keep within the area of observable fact and to ask what we find there and whether the findings provide any warrant for affirming the reality of love.

Call this principle of integration by the religiously nearer names of love and God if you can (as I both can and do) and ask what it means in terms of fact — or facts, I should say, because it rests upon a careful thinking together of several sets or areas or levels of fact. It is, I suppose, humanly impossible to escape from seeming to reason from and by analogy in matters like this, and we are in danger of doing just that when we use such words as " sets," " areas," " levels." Yet they, or some other more adequate word, are essential ways of indicating varying degrees of immediacy and complexity in our apprehension of fact. The further meaning of this will be apparent as we discuss the three levels of fact in which we find definite evidence of the reality of an integrative process upon which we base the philosophical principle of integration as a possible clue to the deepest workings of the universe.

The physical scientist would leap out of his laboratory, if not his skin, if you should ask him whether he finds any evidence for believing in the reality of love as a cosmic principle. He would probably reply that he is not concerned with such phenomena; that he studies the elements which are at work in physical reality; that love is the concern of the biologist and the sociologist. Most of us — too many of us — leave him at that point, which, strictly speaking, is precisely the point at which we should stick to him " closer than a brother " and ask him what it is he has found out about the character and behavior of these elements. In answer to this inquiry, he sooner or later will haul out the table of elements and begin to talk about the properties of various ones like hydrogen, oxygen, carbon and the rest. He will talk about the valence of each one, explaining that valence is its capacity for entering into combination with other elements. For example, hydrogen has a valence of 1, oxygen of 2, and carbon of 4. He will explain further that elements are always found in combinations of varying complexity — at least until they are separated by laboratory processes. As he talks it will become increasingly clear that these elements possess some amazing properties not fully explained by the simple statement that they have such-and-such valence or atomic weight. Once they get in certain combinations, new properties begin to emerge. The stock example of this is that particularly fortunate combination of hydrogen and oxygen in the water molecule, H_2O, which, while composed of two atoms of hydrogen and one of oxygen, is certainly more than a mere sum of what we knew about them prior to this particular combination. In other words, this combination has properties peculiar to itself, properties which belong to hydrogen and oxygen only relative to a certain combination, namely, H_2O. The combination has a nature of its own as truly as either of its components prior to combination. Hydrogen by itself is not wet, and neither is oxygen, but put them together in the proper relationship and one of the properties of the relationship is wetness.

One of the reasons for the amazing development of applied science is the extreme skill with which laboratories have been able to develop processes whereby new and stable combinations of elements can be brought into existence. But for the moment we are not concerned with such man-made products; we are trying to get an idea of the groundwork of the universe in which we live and of which we are integral parts. The exact scientist points out that elements-in-combination constitutes this foundation. This is true not only of inorganic matter but of organic matter as well. The cell, the unit of life, is composed of elements in a definite combination. Once your foot is on this lowest rung in the ladder of life-forms you can move with decision to the very top. Cells in combination form tissues; tissues in combination form organs; and so on up the ladder until we come to selves in combination forming a society. Whether all these combinations come into existence by design or chance is a moot question among students, but there is no argument about the plain fact that some of them are stable and some are not, some last and some disappear.

What the scientist talks about when he talks about valence, combinations and development is the basis in fact for the assertion that a process of integration is plainly discernible in this universe *as known*. While there is much about this process that we do not know — the truth of the matter being that we do not know how much or how little we know relative to all that can be known —,what we do know provides all the warrant we need for the confident assertion that we are being true to facts when we say that a principle of integration is rooted in our knowledge of fact.

On the second level of facts supporting such a principle we find love, meaning the affectional relationship between persons symbolized by the commitment of the whole person. This is the process, the reality, which binds persons into the relationships of marriage, home and family. But it is far from being — nor can it conceivably be — the only relationship which exists between and among persons. We know from our own experience that several other potential if not actual kinds of relationship are possible. Persons can ignore each other — this is probably the meagerest kind of relationship possible. Or they can tolerate each other by means of a "live and let live" attitude but assume no further mutual responsibility than that. Or they can hate each other — which after all is one of the most intensely personal relationships imaginable — and seek the destruction of each other. Or they can recognize their need for each other in creative relationships and become friends — friendship meaning just that, a merging of life in terms of certain interests and activities. Of course there are all gradations of friendship, and in its higher reaches it is one of the rarest experiences open to humanity. If the two persons concerned are man and woman, still another relationship is open to them, that of love, which is a merging of life in terms of all activities and interests, both present and future. I am not saying that such relationships proceed with escalator-like regularity from one stage to another. What I am saying is this: On the level of personal relationships the process of creativity is plainly discernible in the growth of values in personal relationships. This growth is real, not fictional; it is the way the process of integration manifests itself on the human level in personal relations. Because the process of integration is as real here as it is in the areas studied by the physical scientists it is possible for us to affirm that love, as the principle of integration, is rooted in a whole range of known facts.

When we look more carefully at the social nature of the self and study the processes by which a society takes and keeps form we discover still another area of fact in which the process of integration is clearly a phase of reality. Professor

Emory Bogardus charts the direction of our study when he writes: "Human beings begin life as simple organic units and develop into personalities with complex spiritual qualities." [2] Probably no social psychologist has done more to analyze the way in which a self develops than George Herbert Mead, whose main ideas have recently been made available in *Mind, Self and Society*.[3] It is enough for our purpose to note his conclusion that the self grows to selfhood by an intensely social process. To be sure, it begins its career as a psychophysical organism with as yet undetermined capacities. More precise knowledge of what these are will come from the scientist, not from the philosopher, and it does not help much to have the latter do a lot of guessing about it. Indeed too much of the discussion over environment versus heredity is carried on by persons not at all equipped to render a reliable judgment. We have to take the infant at birth as a psychophysical organism whose personality, whose self, is going to grow through a long, constant social process, and while it will grow faster in earlier years there is no reason to say that it is ever really beyond the possibility of further growth. The psychophysical organism is the *given;* the self, the personality, is the *given as socialized* through the experiences of living. Probably the most revealing thing about the given, in this case, is the potentiality of socialization — and to the best of our knowledge this potentiality hovers over every normal psychophysical organism at birth. There is, then, ample warrant for asserting that the process of integration can be seen in the growth of the self.

Naturally, what we have been saying is as revelatory of the character of society as of the self. For society is the environment which is most active in the growth of the self. We are beginning to appreciate how pervasive and complex a fact it is. It is not, as Hobbes thought, a kind of contractual arrangement whereby individuals decide to live together. Nor is it an optional device for dispelling lonesomeness. Society is one of the elemental facts in human life, and it is futile to ask which came first, self or society. Each without the other is a meaningless abstraction; they are never found separately in reality. But we know enough about the history of any given society to know that it, too, is subject to the law or trend of development. What were once simple tribal societies have over several thousand years become complex agricultural or highly industrialized and urbanized societies. In the days of Homer, the Greeks were loosely organized around various sections of the Achaean peninsula. Six hundred years later the Golden Age of Pericles saw a highly urbanized civilization, with laws, government, art, education, and a general culture so different from that of earlier days as to be almost unrecognizable for a development thereof. It is hard for us to realize the change that has come over Japan as a society in the last one hundred years. A simple, self-sufficient society living close to the land and the sea has suddenly become one of the great powers of the earth, highly self-conscious, with a sense of world mission familiar to students of Anglo-Saxon history, and dangerously urbanized and industrialized. Our Bible can be read, as Shailer Mathews was fond of pointing out, as a document which reveals the growth of Hebrew society from the stage of tribalism to that of an agricultural community which dreamed dreams of world destiny and mission.

We do not yet know whether it is possible for the history of any society to end otherwise than in tragedy. Spengler and Toynbee are not very optimistic about the possibility of a happier outcome. But the hope will not down that somehow we shall find a way to bring into being a society capable of so adjusting itself to the nature of the universe as to be able to survive the ravages of time. While there is much that we do not know about how this can and should be done, the general outline of a society that has a chance to survive is pretty well recognized. It will be one which seeks to realize what Archbishop Temple has termed the "commonwealth of values," or, to call it by its traditional names, the "Kingdom of

God" or the "brotherhood of man." Even though modern
history is the "one bloody lump" Lenin once called it; even
though there is empirical warrant for Keats's phrase, "the gi-
ant agony of mankind," there is still reason to believe that we
are not wholly cut off from achieving the distant goal of world
brotherhood. That we are going to have to do a lot of replan-
ning as well as repenting is too obvious to detain us with argument. The foundation for a world order has been laid
by the very processes of communication, transportation and
travel that have made the world into a neighborhood. The
crucial question before us was memorably phrased by Dr.
Harry Emerson Fosdick: "Are we going to be able to make
this neighborhood into a brotherhood?"

The first step in that direction is to develop a sense of oneness with the rest of mankind. All our current talk about
collective security overlooks one basic consideration: collective security begins as collective concern. And collective concern begins as consciousness of kind or sense of mutuality.
We have taken great strides in this direction already. The
very speed with which war now engulfs the whole world is
terrible proof of the fact that we are too deeply interdependent with each other ever to attempt to live separately again.
But, just as it has been possible for peoples who have fought
several wars finally to learn to trust each other in certain basic
ways, there is no known reason why the nations in the contemporary world cannot learn to trust each other. To this
end there must be held before them a vision of a world society, a "commonwealth of values," in which the rights and
privileges of each will be safeguarded. If and to the degree
that such a world order comes into being, it will be a further
development of the process of integration which has been trying to bring it into existence in the past, only to be balked by
rebellious materials. To the thoughtful observer, it is not impossible to fit the high mortality rate of societies into the general world view. Their death is just what you would expect
in a moral world, one in which you either move upward by

creative steps or slide downward to extinction by attempting to ignore the thrust toward creative universality and mutuality which seems to be an integral aspect and requirement of the process of integration.

It is against some such background as this that the contemporary philosopher of religion reaffirms the ancient belief that God is love. When he makes this affirmation he is not flying in the face of facts; he is paying scrupulous regard to facts. He is not flinging a defiant faith in the face of a hostile universe; he is gearing in with what seems to him to be the strongest tendency, trend or process in the universe *as known and experienced.* When we as Christian preachers affirm the reality of love and bid men and nations order their lives according to its dictates, we are not asking them to pursue a fanciful ideal; we are asking them to face facts. We are asking them to face the profound fact that there is no such thing in this universe as a separate value, or a separate self, or a separate society.

The great values of truth, beauty and goodness are so inextricably interwoven with each other that a careful development of the meaning of any one of them finally involves all three. This fact, which seems to have eluded the Greek thinkers as well as a good many contemporary ones, is the meaning of the Christian concept of love. You and I as individual selves and persons have great freedom in our interrelations one with another, but that freedom stops short of our being able to deny and disown our dependence upon and interdependence with each other. We are bound together in one bundle of life. The complete history of any given society may well spend most of its time telling of certain events linked together in the folklore, traditions and institutions of the group, but if it is really complete it will draw in as of great importance many factors usually ignored or slighted, such as the natural resources of the country, contacts with other peoples, and a conscious religious response to what Whitehead has called " the lure of the beyond."

It is the carefully considered contention of the Christian faith that we must finally come to terms with the reality of an integrative process which sweeps through the entire universe, from atom to star, from man to society; a process which knits the human enterprise into the texture of cosmic events; a process known to us by the nearer names of Love and God. It is the further contention of the Christian faith that our clearest insight into the fundamental workings of this process in human relations is to be found in the life and teachings of Jesus Christ. For it was he who taught us how truly and deeply God loves the world; it was he who etched upon our conscience the outline of our only adequate response to this love.✤

REFERENCES

1 Hartshorne, *Man's Vision of God*, p. ix.

2 Emory Bogardus, *Fundamentals of Social Psychology* (New York: Century Co., 1924), p. 3.

3 George Herbert Mead, *Mind, Self and Society* (Chicago: University of Chicago Press, 1934).

Appendix

LLLLLLLLLLLLLLLLLLLLLLLLLLLLLLLLLLLr

Selections from Plato*

THE SPEECH OF DIOTIMA
FROM THE *SYMPOSIUM*

[Benjamin Jowett begins his introduction to the *Symposium*
with this statement: "Of all the works of Plato the *Symposium*
is the most perfect in form, and may be truly thought to contain more than any commentator has ever dreamed of." As
in all Platonic dialogues the thought proceeds in a leisurely
manner. Plato is touring the various interpretations of the
nature or meaning of love. But, as always, he is a sharp-eyed,
keenly inquisitive tourist who is out to get completely ac-
quainted with each explanation. A tropical profusion of
metaphors and similes and all manner of distinctions dot the
pages of this dialogue.

The setting for the discussion of love is at a banquet.
Plato must have reveled in such gatherings if we may judge
by the way in which he sketches this one.

The passage quoted in the following pages is the famous
discourse on love which Diotima, a wise woman of Mantineia,
had given to Socrates and which he, in turn, shares with his
fellows at the banquet. It should be read many times in order
to appreciate its richness. It comes closer than any other passage in Plato's writings to discovering the interrelatedness of
values which Christian thought was later to discover and exalt
as God. Notice how Plato keeps moving from beauty to love,
to the good, to happiness, to truth. Here, lying unrecognized
in his hands, was the clue to the fundamental nature of the
universe, the cohesive character of values, which undergirds
the Christian insistence that "God is love." The climax of

* These selections are taken from *The Dialogues of Plato*, translated into
English by Benjamin Jowett, M.A. 2 vols. (New York: Random House, 1937.
Copyright Oxford University Press).

Plato's thought comes at a different point however — a vision of "the sea of beauty." Which, I suppose, illustrates better than anything else the essential difference between his thought and Christian thought.]

Socrates. "And now, taking my leave of you, I will rehearse a tale of love which I heard from Diotima of Mantineia, a woman wise in this and in many other kinds of knowledge, who in the days of old, when the Athenians offered sacrifice before the coming of the plague, delayed the disease ten years. She was my instructress in the art of love, and I shall repeat to you what she said to me, beginning with the admissions made by Agathon, which are nearly if not quite the same which I made to the wise woman when she questioned me: I think that this will be the easiest way, and I shall take both parts myself as well as I can. As you, Agathon, suggested, I must speak first of the being and nature of Love, and then of his works. First I said to her in nearly the same words which he used to me, that Love was a mighty god, and likewise fair; and she proved to me as I proved to him that, by my own showing, Love was neither fair nor good. 'What do you mean, Diotima,' I said, 'is love then evil and foul?' 'Hush,' she cried; 'must that be foul which is not fair?' 'Certainly,' I said. 'And is that which is not wise, ignorant? do you not see that there is a mean between wisdom and ignorance?' 'And what may that be?' I said. 'Right opinion,' she replied; 'which, as you know, being incapable of giving a reason, is not knowledge (for how can knowledge be devoid of reason? nor again, ignorance, for neither can ignorance attain the truth), but is clearly something which is a mean between ignorance and wisdom.' 'Quite true,' I replied. 'Do not then insist,' she said, 'that what is not fair is of necessity foul, or what is not good evil; or infer that because love is not fair and good he is therefore foul and evil; for he is in a mean between them.' 'Well,' I said, 'Love is surely admitted by all to be a great god.' 'By those who know or by those who do not know?' 'By all.' 'And how, Socrates,' she said with a smile, 'can Love be acknowledged to be a great god by those who say that he is not a god at all?' 'And who are they?' I said. 'You and I are two of them,' she replied. 'How can that be?' I said. 'It is quite intelligible,' she replied; 'for you yourself would acknowledge that the gods are happy and fair — of course you would — would you dare to say that any god was not?' 'Certainly not,' I replied. 'And you mean by the happy, those who are the possessors of things good or fair?' 'Yes.' 'And you admitted that Love, because he was in want, desires those good and fair things of which he is in want?' 'Yes, I did.' 'But how can he be a god who has no portion in what is either good or fair?' 'Impossible.' 'Then you see that you also deny the divinity of Love.'

'What then is Love?' I asked; 'Is he mortal?' 'No.' 'What then?' 'As in the former instance, he is neither mortal nor immortal, but in a mean between the two.' 'What is he, Diotima?' 'He is a great spirit, and like all spirits he is intermediate between the divine and the mortal.' 'And what,' I said, 'is his power?' 'He interprets,' she replied, 'between gods and men, conveying and taking across to the gods the prayers and sacrifices of men, and to men the commands and replies of the gods; he is the mediator who spans the chasm which divides them, and therefore in him all is bound together, and through him the arts of the prophet and the priest, their sacrifices and mysteries and charms, and all prophecy and incantation, find their way. For God mingles not with man; but through Love all the intercourse and converse of god with man, whether awake or asleep, is carried on. The wisdom which understands this is spiritual; all other wisdom, such as that of arts and handicrafts, is mean and vulgar. Now these spirits or intermediate powers are many and diverse, and one of them is Love.' 'And who,' I said, 'was his father, and who his mother?' 'The tale,' she said, 'will take time; nevertheless I will tell you. On the birthday of Aphrodite there was a feast of the gods, at which the god Poros or Plenty, who is the son of Metis or Discretion, was one of the guests. When the feast was over, Penia or Poverty, as the manner is on such occasions, came about the doors to beg. Now Plenty, who was the worse for nectar (there was no wine in those days), went into the garden of Zeus and fell into a heavy sleep; and Poverty considering her own straitened circumstances, plotted to have a child by him, and accordingly she lay down at his side and conceived Love, who partly because he is naturally a lover of the beautiful, and because Aphrodite is herself beautiful, and also because he was born on her birthday, is her follower and attendant. And as his parentage is, so also are his fortunes. In the first place he is always poor, and anything but tender and fair, as the many imagine him; and he is rough and squalid, and has no shoes, nor a house to dwell in; on the bare earth exposed he lies under the open heaven, in the streets, or at the doors of houses, taking his rest; and like his mother he is always in distress. Like his father too, whom he also partly resembles, he is always plotting against the fair and good; he is bold, enterprising, strong, a mighty hunter, always weaving some intrigue or other, keen in the pursuit of wisdom, fertile in resources; a philosopher at all times, terrible as an enchanter, sorcerer, sophist. He is by nature neither mortal nor immortal, but alive and flourishing at one moment when he is in plenty, and dead at another moment, and again alive by reason of his father's nature. But that which is always flowing in is always flowing out, and so he is never in want and never in wealth; and, further, he is in a mean between ignorance and knowledge. The truth of the matter is this: No god is a philosopher or seeker after wisdom, for he is wise already; nor does any man who is wise seek after wisdom. Neither do the ignorant seek after wisdom. For herein is the evil of ignorance, that he who is neither good nor wise is nevertheless satisfied with himself: he has no desire for that of which he feels no want.' 'But who then, Diotima,' I said, 'are the lovers of wisdom, if they are neither the wise nor the foolish?' 'A child may answer that question,' she replied; 'they are those who are in a mean between the two; Love is one of them. For wisdom is a most beautiful thing, and Love is of the beautiful; and therefore Love is also a philosopher or lover of wisdom, and being a lover of wisdom is in a mean between the wise and the ignorant. And of this too his birth is the cause; for his father is wealthy and wise, and his mother poor and foolish. Such, my dear Socrates, is the nature of the spirit Love. The error in your conception of him was very natural, and as I imagine from what you say, has arisen out of a confusion of love and the beloved, which made you think that love was all beautiful. For the beloved is the truly beautiful, and delicate, and perfect, and blessed; but the principle of love is of another nature, and is such as I have described.'

I said: 'O thou stranger woman, thou sayest well; but, assuming Love to be such as you say, what is the use of him to men?'

'That, Socrates,' she replied, 'I will attempt to unfold: of his nature and birth I have already spoken; and you acknowledge that
love is of the beautiful. But some one will say: Of the beautiful
in what, Socrates and Diotima? — or rather let me put the question more clearly, and ask: When a man loves the beautiful, what
does he desire?' I answered her 'That the beautiful may be his.'
'Still,' she said, 'the answer suggests a further question: What is
given by the possession of beauty?' 'To what you have asked,'
I replied, 'I have no answer ready.' 'Then,' she said, 'let me put
the word "good" in the place of the beautiful, and repeat the
question once more: If he who loves loves the good, what is it
then that he loves?' 'The possession of the good,' I said. 'And
what does he gain who possesses the good?' 'Happiness,' I replied; 'there is less difficulty in answering that question.' 'Yes,'
she said, 'the happy are made happy by the acquisition of good
things. Nor is there any need to ask why a man desires happiness;
the answer is already final.' 'You are right,' I said. 'And is this
wish and this desire common to all? and do all men always desire
their own good, or only some men? — what say you?' 'All men,'
I replied; 'the desire is common to all.' 'Why, then,' she rejoined,
'are not all men, Socrates, said to love, but only some of them?
whereas you say that all men are always loving the same things.'
'I myself wonder,' I said, 'why this is.' 'There is nothing to wonder at,' she replied; 'the reason is that one part of love is separated
off and receives the name of the whole, but the other parts have
other names.' 'Give an illustration,' I said. She answered me as
follows: 'There is poetry, which, as you know, is complex and
manifold. All creation or passage of non-being into being is poetry
or making, and the processes of all art are creative; and the masters of arts are all poets or makers.' 'Very true.' 'Still,' she said,
'you know that they are not called poets, but have other names;
only that portion of the art which is separated off from the rest,
and is concerned with music and metre, is termed poetry, and they
who possess poetry in this sense of the word are called poets.'
'Very true,' I said. 'And the same holds of love. For you may
say generally that all desire of good and happiness is only the
great and subtle power of love; but they who are drawn towards
him by any other path, whether the path of money-making or
gymnastics or philosophy, are not called lovers— the name of the

whole is appropriated to those whose affection takes one form only — they alone are said to love, or to be lovers.' ' I dare say,' I replied, ' that you are right.' ' Yes,' she added, ' and you hear people say that lovers are seeking for their other half; but I say that they are seeking neither for the half of themselves, nor for the whole, unless the half or the whole be also a good. And they will cut off their own hands and feet and cast them away, if they are evil; for they love not what is their own, unless perchance there be some one who calls what belongs to him the good, and what belongs to another the evil. For there is nothing which men love but the good. Is there anything?' ' Certainly, I should say, that there is nothing.' ' Then,' she said, ' the simple truth is, that men love the good.' ' Yes,' I said. ' To which must be added that they love the possession of the good?' ' Yes, that must be added.' ' And not only the possession, but the everlasting possession of the good?' ' That must be added too.' ' Then love,' she said, ' may be described generally as the love of the everlasting possession of the good?' ' That is most true.'

' Then if this be the nature of love, can you tell me further,' she said, ' what is the manner of the pursuit? what are they doing who show all this eagerness and heat which is called love? and what is the object which they have in view? Answer me.' ' Nay, Diotima,' I replied, ' if I had known, I should not have wondered at your wisdom, neither should I have come to learn from you about this very matter.' ' Well,' she said, ' I will teach you: — The object which they have in view is birth in beauty, whether of body or soul.' ' I do not understand you,' I said; ' the oracle requires an explanation.' ' I will make my meaning clearer,' she replied. ' I mean to say, that all men are bringing to the birth in their bodies and in their souls. There is a certain age at which human nature is desirous of procreation — procreation which must be in beauty and not in deformity; and this procreation is the union of man and woman, and is a divine thing; for conception and generation are an immortal principle in the mortal creature, and in the inharmonious they can never be. But the deformed is always inharmonious with the divine, and the beautiful harmonious. Beauty, then, is the destiny or goddess of parturition who presides at birth, and therefore, when approaching beauty, the conceiving power is propitious, and diffusive, and benign, and begets and bears fruit: at the sight of ugliness she frowns and contracts and has a sense of pain, and turns away, and shrivels up, and not without a pang refrains from conception. And this is the reason why, when the hour of conception arrives, and the teeming nature is full, there is such a flutter and ecstasy about beauty whose approach is the alleviation of the pain of travail. For love, Socrates, is not, as you imagine, the love of the beautiful only.' 'What then?' 'The love of generation and of birth in beauty.' 'Yes,' I said. 'Yes, indeed,' she replied. 'But why of generation?' 'Because to the mortal creature, generation is a sort of eternity and immortality,' she replied; 'and if, as has been already admitted, love is of the everlasting possession of the good, all men will necessarily desire immortality together with good: Wherefore love is of immortality.'

All this she taught me at various times when she spoke of love. And I remember her once saying to me, 'What is the cause, Socrates, of love, and the attendant desire? See you not how all animals, birds, as well as beasts, in their desire of procreation, are in agony when they take the infection of love, which begins with the desire of union; whereto is added the care of offspring, on whose behalf the weakest are ready to battle against the strongest even to the uttermost, and to die for them, and will let themselves be tormented with hunger or suffer anything in order to maintain their young. Man may be supposed to act thus from reason; but why should animals have these passionate feelings? Can you tell me why?' Again I replied that I did not know. She said to me: 'And do you expect ever to become a master in the art of love, if you do not know this?' 'But I have told you already, Diotima, that my ignorance is the reason why I come to you; for I am conscious that I want a teacher; tell me then the cause of this and of the other mysteries of love.' 'Marvel not,' she said, 'if you believe that love is of the immortal, as we have several times acknowledged; for here again, and on the same principle too, the mortal nature is seeking as far as is possible to be everlasting and immortal: and this is only to be attained by generation, because generation always leaves behind a new existence in the place of the old. Nay even in the life of the same individual there is succession and not absolute unity: a man is called the same, and yet in the short interval which elapses between youth and age, and in which every animal is said to have life and identity, he is undergoing a perpetual process of loss and reparation — hair, flesh, bones, blood, and the whole body are always changing. Which is true not only of the body, but also of the soul, whose habits, tempers, opinions, desires, pleasures, pains, fears, never remain the same in any one of us, but are always coming and going; and equally true of knowledge, and what is still more surprising to us mortals, not only do the sciences in general spring up and decay, so that in respect of them we are never the same; but each of them individually experiences a like change. For what is implied in the word "recollection," but the departure of knowledge, which is ever being forgotten, and is renewed and preserved by recollection, and appears to be the same although in reality new, according to that law of succession by which all mortal things are preserved, not absolutely the same, but by substitution, the old worn-out mortality leaving another new and similar existence behind — unlike the divine, which is always the same and not another? And in this way, Socrates, the mortal body, or mortal anything, partakes of immortality; but the immortal in another way. Marvel not then at the love which all men have of their offspring; for that universal love and interest is for the sake of immortality.'

I was astonished at her words, and said: 'Is this really true, O thou wise Diotima?' And she answered with all the authority of an accomplished sophist: 'Of that, Socrates, you may be assured; — think only of the ambition of men, and you will wonder at the senselessness of their ways, unless you consider how they are stirred by the love of an immortality of fame. They are ready to run all risks greater far than they would have run for their children, and to spend money and undergo any sort of toil, and even to die, for the sake of leaving behind them a name which shall be eternal. Do you imagine that Alcestis would have died to save Admetus, or Achilles to avenge Patroclus, or your own Codrus in order to preserve the kingdom for his sons, if they had not imagined that the memory of their virtues, which still survives among us, would be immortal? Nay,' she said, 'I am persuaded that all men do all things, and the better they are the more they do them, in hope of the glorious fame of immortal virtue; for they desire the immortal.

'Those who are pregnant in the body only, betake themselves to women and beget children — this is the character of their love;

their offspring, as they hope, will preserve their memory and give them the blessedness and immortality which they desire in the future. But souls which are pregnant — for there certainly are men who are more creative in their souls than in their bodies — conceive that which is proper for the soul to conceive or contain. And what are these conceptions? — wisdom and virtue in general. And such creators are poets and all artists who are deserving of the name inventor. But the greatest and fairest sort of wisdom by far is that which is concerned with the ordering of states and families, and which is called temperance and justice. And he who in youth has the seed of these implanted in him and is himself inspired, when he comes to maturity desires to beget and generate. He wanders about seeking beauty that he may beget offspring — for in deformity he will beget nothing — and naturally embraces the beautiful rather than the deformed body; above all when he finds a fair and noble and well-nurtured soul, he embraces the two in one person, and to such an one he is full of speech about virtue and the nature and pursuits of a good man; and he tries to educate him; and at the touch of the beautiful which is ever present to his memory, even when absent, he brings forth that which he had conceived long before, and in company with him tends that which he brings forth; and they are married by a far nearer tie and have a closer friendship than those who beget mortal children, for the children who are their common offspring are fairer and more immortal. Who, when he thinks of Homer and Hesiod and other great poets, would not rather have their children than ordinary human ones? Who would not emulate them in the creation of children such as theirs, which have preserved their memory and given them everlasting glory? Or who would not have such children as Lycurgus left behind him to be the saviors, not only of Lacedaemon, but of Hellas, as one may say? There is Solon, too, who is the revered father of Athenian laws; and many others there are in many other places, both among Hellenes and barbarians, who have given to the world many noble works, and have been the parents of virtue of every kind; and many temples have been raised in their honor for the sake of children such as theirs; which were never raised in honor of any one, for the sake of his mortal children.

    ' These are the lesser mysteries of love, into which even you,

Socrates, may enter; to the greater and more hidden ones which are the crown of these, and to which, if you pursue them in a right spirit, they will lead, I know not whether you will be able to attain. But I will do my utmost to inform you, and do you follow if you can. For he who would proceed aright in this matter should begin in youth to visit beautiful forms; and first, if he be guided by his instructor aright, to love one such form only — out of that he should create fair thoughts; and soon he will of himself perceive that the beauty of one form is akin to the beauty of another; and then if beauty of form in general is his pursuit, how foolish would he be not to recognize that the beauty in every form is one and the same! And when he perceives this he will abate his violent love of the one, which he will despise and deem a small thing, and will become a lover of all beautiful forms; in the next stage he will consider that the beauty of the mind is more honorable than the beauty of the outward form. So that if a virtuous soul have but a little comeliness, he will be content to love and tend him, and will search out and bring to the birth thoughts which may improve the young, until he is compelled to contemplate and see the beauty of institutions and laws, and to understand that the beauty of them all is of one family, and that personal beauty is a trifle; and after laws and institutions he will go on to the sciences, that he may see their beauty, being not like a servant in love with the beauty of one youth or man or institution, himself a slave mean and narrow-minded, but drawing towards and contemplating the vast sea of beauty, he will create many fair and noble thoughts and notions in boundless love of wisdom; until on that shore he grows and waxes strong, and at last the vision is revealed to him of a single science, which is the science of beauty everywhere. To this I will proceed; please to give me your very best attention:

' He who has been instructed thus far in the things of love, and who has learned to see the beautiful in due order and succession, when he comes toward the end will suddenly perceive a nature of wondrous beauty (and this, Socrates, is the final cause of all our former toils) — a nature which in the first place is everlasting, not growing and decaying, or waxing and waning; secondly, not fair in one point of view and foul in another, or at one time or in one relation or at one place fair, at another time or in another relation or at another place foul, as if fair to some and foul to others, or in

the likeness of a face or hands or any other part of the bodily
frame, or in any form of speech or knowledge, or existing in any
other being, as for example, in an animal, or in heaven, or in
earth, or in any other place; but beauty absolute, separate, simple, and everlasting, which without diminution and without increase, or any change, is imparted to the ever-growing and perishing beauties of all other things. He who from these ascending
under the influence of true love, begins to perceive that beauty, is
not far from the end. And the true order of going, or being led by
another, to the things of love, is to begin from the beauties of
earth and mount upwards for the sake of that other beauty, using
these as steps only, and from one going on to two, and from two
to all fair forms, and from fair forms to fair practices, and from
fair practices to fair notions, until from fair notions he arrives at
the notion of absolute beauty, and at last knows what the essence
of beauty is. This, my dear Socrates,' said the stranger of Mantineia, ' is that life above all others which man should live, in the
contemplation of beauty absolute; a beauty which if you once beheld, you would see not to be after the measure of gold, and gar-
ments, and fair boys and youths, whose presence now entrances
you; and you and many a one would be content to live seeing them
only and conversing with them without meat or drink, if that were
possible — you only want to look at them and to be with them.
But what if man had eyes to see the true beauty — the divine
beauty, I mean, pure and clear and unalloyed, not clogged with
the pollutions of mortality and all the colors and vanities of human
life — thither looking, and holding converse with the true beauty
simple and divine? Remember how in that communion only, be-
holding beauty with the eye of the mind, he will be enabled to
bring forth, not images of beauty, but realities (for he has hold
not of an image but of a reality), and bringing forth and nourish-
ing true virtue to become the friend of God and be immortal, if
mortal man may. Would that be an ignoble life? '

Such, Phaedrus — and I speak not only to you, but to all of you
— were the words of Diotima; and I am persuaded of their truth.
And being persuaded of them, I try to persuade others, that in the
attainment of this end human nature will not easily find a helper
better than love. And therefore, also, I say that every man ought
to honor him as I myself honor him, and walk in his ways, and ex-

hort others to do the same, and praise the power and spirit of love according to the measure of my ability now and ever.

The words which I have spoken, you, Phaedrus, may call an encomium of love, or anything else which you please.

(*Vol. I, pp. 327–35*)

FROM THE PRELUDE OF THE *TIMAEUS*

[The *Timaeus* finds Plato grappling, as every speculative philosopher must, with the problems of cosmology. What, he is inquiring, is the essential pattern of the world? How can we account for its existence? How can we possess knowledge of it? These and related queries launch the discussion in this dialogue, which, by any manner of reckoning, is one of the most difficult of them all. Yet its wisdom seems perennially fresh. Of it, Professor A. N. Whitehead has observed that all subsequent philosophy is a matter of dropping footnotes to it! Timaeus carries the standard in the discussion, an honor usually accorded Socrates when he is depicted as being present. Plato's ability to write movingly about the nature and work of God as the Creator of the universe is conveyed by the following section.]

Timaeus. All men, Socrates, who have any degree of right feeling, at the beginning of every enterprise, whether small or great, always call upon God. And we, too, who are going to discourse of the nature of the universe, how created or how existing without creation, if we be not altogether out of our wits, must invoke the aid of Gods and Goddesses and pray that our words may be acceptable to them and consistent with themselves. Let this, then, be our invocation of the Gods, to which I add an exhortation of myself to speak in such manner as will be most intelligible to you, and will most accord with my own intent.

First then in my judgment, we must make a distinction and ask, What is that which always is and has no becoming; and what is that which is always becoming and never is? That which is apprehended by intelligence and reason is always in the same state; but that which is conceived by opinion with the help of sensation and without reason, is always in a process of becoming and perishing and never really is. Now everything that becomes or is created must of necessity be created by some cause, for without a cause nothing can be created. The work of the creator, whenever he looks to the unchangeable and fashions the form and nature of his work after an unchangeable pattern, must necessarily be made fair and perfect; but when he looks to the created only, and uses a created pattern, it is not fair or perfect. Was the heaven then or the world, whether called by this or by any other more appropriate name — assuming the name, I am asking a question which has to be asked at the beginning of an enquiry about anything — was the world, I say, always in existence and without beginning? or created, and had it a beginning? Created, I reply, being visible and tangible and having a body, and therefore sensible; and all sensible things are apprehended by opinion and sense and are in a process of creation and created. Now that which is created must, as we affirm, of necessity be created by a cause. But the father and maker of all this universe is past finding out; and even if we found him, to tell of him to all men would be impossible. And there is still a question to be asked about him: Which of the patterns had the artificer in view when he made the world, — the pattern of the unchangeable, or of that which is created? If the world be indeed fair and the artificer good, it is manifest that he must have looked to that which is eternal; but if what cannot be said without blasphemy is true, then to the created pattern. Every one will see that he must have looked to the eternal; for the world is the fairest of creations and he is the best of causes. And having been created in this way, the world has been framed in the likeness of that which is apprehended by reason and mind and is unchangeable, and must therefore of necessity, if this is admitted, be a copy of something. Now it is all-important that the beginning of everything should be according to nature. And in speaking of the copy and the original we may assume that words are akin to the matter which they describe; when they relate to the lasting and permanent and intelligible, they ought to be lasting and unalterable, and, as far as their nature allows, irrefutable and immovable — nothing less. But when they express only the copy or likeness and not the eternal things themselves, they need only be likely and analogous to the real words. As being is to becoming, so is truth to belief. If then, Socrates, amid the many opinions about the gods and the generation of the universe, we are not able to give notions which are altogether and in every respect exact and consistent with one another, do not be surprised. Enough, if we adduce probabilities as likely as any others; for we must remember that I who am the speaker, and you who are the judges, are only mortal men, and we ought to accept the tale which is probable and enquire no further.

Soc. Excellent, Timaeus; and we will do precisely as you bid us. The prelude is charming, and is already accepted by us — may we beg of you to proceed to the strain?

Tim. Let me tell you then why the creator made this world of generation. He was good, and the good can never have any jealousy of anything. And being free from jealousy, he desired that all things should be as like himself as they could be. This is in the truest sense the origin of creation and of the world, as we shall do well in believing on the testimony of wise men: God desired that all things should be good and nothing bad, so far as this was attainable. Wherefore also finding the whole visible sphere not at rest, but moving in an irregular and disorderly fashion, out of disorder he brought order, considering that this was in every way better than the other. Now the deeds of the best could never be or have been other than the fairest; and the creator, reflecting on the things which are by nature visible, found that no unintelligent creature taken as a whole was fairer than the intelligent taken as a whole; and that intelligence could not be present in anything which was devoid of soul. For which reason, when he was framing the universe, he put intelligence in soul, and soul in body, that he might be the creator of a work which was by nature fairest and best. Wherefore, using the language of probability, we may say that the world became a living creature truly endowed with soul and intelligence by the providence of God.

(*Vol. II, pp. 12–14*)

FROM THE *LAWS*, BOOK X

[Plato was a practical as well as a theoretical theologian. He not only wanted his ideas about God to be couched in clear, persuasive terms; he also wanted them respected and honored by men. The following excerpt from his last great work, the *Laws,* exhibits a mood not unlike that found among some of the more enlightened inquisitors of later ages. Men should be persuaded to respect the gods if possible. But if they refuse to yield to persuasion and persist in their unbelief they are to be punished. Offenders are to be divided into three classes according to the enormity of their crime of unbelief. Innocent offenders are to be imprisoned; more serious ones are to be executed; the most dangerous ones — " those who believe that the gods favor the wicked in return for their gifts — shall be imprisoned during life, and never again hold intercourse with their fellows, and when they die, their bodies shall be cast beyond the borders."

Against this background, it is not difficult to make the point that the aged Plato is taking his theology seriously and means to have others do likewise. He is out to prove the existence and the supreme morality of the gods. The Sophists — shrewd, skeptical teachers who thronged Athens in Plato's youth — had doubted if not ridiculed both attributes of the gods — their reality and their morality. You will want to measure Plato's theological efforts against those of the intellectual giants of the Christian tradition: Origen, Augustine, Aquinas, Calvin. As you do this, it will become apparent that philosophy by herself is unable to fashion the Christian idea of God. Prophetic, mystical religious experience has revealed and plumbed depths of meaning which philosophy alone has not found. But even so, when a mind like Plato works at theology it is the part of wisdom to give undivided attention. If

130

Origen, Augustine and Aquinas paid him that honor, can any Christian theologian do less?]

Cleinias. But is there any difficulty in proving the existence of the Gods?

Athenian. How would you prove it?

Cle. How? In the first place, the earth and the sun, and the stars and the universe, and the fair order of the seasons, and the division of them into years and months, furnish proofs of their existence; and also there is the fact that all Hellenes and barbarians believe in them.

Ath. I fear, my sweet friend, though I will not say that I much regard, the contempt with which the profane will be likely to assail us. For you do not understand the nature of their complaint, and you fancy that they rush into impiety only from a love of sensual pleasure.

Cle. Why, Stranger, what other reason is there?

Ath. One which you who live in a different atmosphere would never guess.

Cle. What is it?

Ath. A very grievous sort of ignorance which is imagined to be the greatest wisdom.

Cle. What do you mean?

Ath. At Athens there are tales preserved in writing which the virtue of your state, as I am informed, refuses to admit. They speak of the Gods in prose as well as verse, and the oldest of them tell of the origin of the heavens and of the world, and not far from the beginning of their story they proceed to narrate the birth of the Gods, and how after they were born they behaved to one another. Whether these stories have in other ways a good or a bad influence, I should not like to be severe upon them, because they are ancient; but, looking at them with reference to the duties of children to their parents, I cannot praise them, or think that they are useful, or at all true. Of the words of the ancients I have nothing more to say; and I should wish to say of them only what is pleasing to the Gods. But as to our younger generation and their wisdom, I cannot let them off when they do mischief. For do but mark the effect of their words: when you and I argue for the existence of the Gods, and produce the sun, moon, stars, and earth, claiming for them a divine being, if we would listen to the afore-said philosophers we should say that they are earth and stones only, which can have no care at all of human affairs, and that all religion is a cooking up of words and a make-believe.

Cle. One such teacher, O Stranger, would be bad enough, and you imply that there are many of them, which is worse.

Ath. Well, then; what shall we say or do? — Shall we assume that some one is accusing us among unholy men, who are trying to escape from the effect of our legislation; and that they say of us — How dreadful that you should legislate on the supposition that there are Gods! Shall we make a defence of ourselves? or shall we leave them and return to our laws, lest the prelude should become longer than the law? For the discourse will certainly extend to great length, if we are to treat the impiously disposed as they desire, partly demonstrating to them at some length the things of which they demand an explanation, partly making them afraid or dissatisfied, and then proceed to the requisite enactments.

Cle. Yes, Stranger; but then how often have we repeated already that on the present occasion there is no reason why brevity should be preferred to length; for who is ' at our heels '? — as the saying goes, and it would be paltry and ridiculous to prefer the shorter to the better. It is a matter of no small consequence, in some way or other to prove that there are Gods, and that they are good, and regard justice more than men do. The demonstration of this would be the best and noblest prelude of all our laws. And therefore, without impatience, and without hurry, let us unreservedly consider the whole matter, summoning up all the power of persuasion which we possess.

Ath. Seeing you thus in earnest, I would fain offer up a prayer that I may succeed: — but I must proceed at once. Who can be calm when he is called upon to prove the existence of the Gods? Who can avoid hating and abhorring the men who are and have been the cause of this argument; I speak of those who will not believe the tales which they have heard as babes and sucklings from their mothers and nurses, repeated by them both in jest and earnest, like charms, who have also heard them in the sacrificial prayers, and seen sights accompanying them, — sights and sounds delightful to children, — and their parents during the sacrifices showing an intense earnestness on behalf of their children and of themselves, and with eager interest talking to the Gods, and beseeching them, as though they were firmly convinced of their existence; who likewise see and hear the prostrations and invocations which are made by Hellenes and barbarians at the rising and setting of the sun and moon, in all the vicissitudes of life, not as if they thought that there were no Gods, but as if there could be no doubt of their existence, and no suspicion of their nonexistence; when men, knowing all these things, despise them on no real grounds, as would be admitted by all who have any particle of intelligence, and when they force us to say what we are now saying, how can any one in gentle terms remonstrate with the like of them, when he has to begin by proving to them the very existence of the Gods? Yet the attempt must be made; for it would be unseemly that one half of mankind should go mad in their lust of pleasure, and the other half in their indignation at such persons. Our address to these lost and perverted natures should not be spoken in passion; let us suppose ourselves to select some one of them, and gently reason with him, smothering our anger: — O my son, we will say to him, you are young, and the advance of time will make you reverse many of the opinions which you now hold. Wait awhile, and do not attempt to judge at present of the highest things; and that is the highest of which you now think nothing — to know the Gods rightly and to live accordingly. And in the first place let me indicate to you one point which is of great importance, and about which I cannot be deceived: — You and your friends are not the first who have held this opinion about the Gods. There have always been persons more or less numerous who have had the same disorder. I have known many of them, and can tell you, that no one who had taken up in youth this opinion, that the Gods do not exist, ever continued in the same until he was old; the two other notions certainly do continue in some cases, but not in many; the notion, I mean, that the Gods exist, but take no heed of human things, and the other notion that they do take heed of them, but are easily propitiated with sacrifices and prayers. As to the opinion about the Gods which may some day become clear to you, I advise you go wait and consider if it be true or not; ask of others, and above all of the legislator. In the meantime take care that you do not offend against the Gods. For the duty of the legislator is and always will be to teach you the truth of these matters.

Cle. Our address, Stranger, thus far, is excellent.

Ath. Quite true, Megillus and Cleinias, but I am afraid that we have unconsciously lighted on a strange doctrine.

Cle. What doctrine do you mean?

Ath. The wisest of all doctrines, in the opinion of many.

Cle. I wish that you would speak plainer.

Ath. The doctrine that all things do become, have become, and will become, some by nature, some by art, and some by chance.

Cle. Is not that true?

Ath. Well, philosophers are probably right; at any rate we may as well follow in their track, and examine what is the meaning of them and their disciples.

Cle. By all means.

Ath. They say that the greatest and fairest things are the work of nature and of chance, the lesser of art, which, receiving from nature the greater and primeval creations, molds and fashions all those lesser works which are generally termed artificial.

Cle. How is that?

Ath. I will explain my meaning still more clearly. They say that fire and water, and earth and air, all exist by nature and chance, and none of them by art, and that as to the bodies which come next in order, — earth, and sun, and moon, and stars, — they have been created by means of these absolutely inanimate existences. The elements are severally moved by chance and some inherent force according to certain affinities among them — of hot with cold, or of dry with moist, or of soft with hard, and according to all the other accidental admixtures of opposites which have been formed by necessity. After this fashion and in this manner the whole heaven has been created, and all that is in the heaven, as well as animals and all plants, and all the seasons come from these elements, not by the action of mind, as they say, or of any God, or from art, but as I was saying, by nature and chance only. Art sprang up afterwards and out of these, mortal and of mortal birth, and produced in play certain images and very partial imitations of the truth, having an affinity to one another, such as music and painting create and their companion arts. And there are other arts which have a serious purpose, and these co-operate with nature, such, for example, as medicine, and husbandry, and gymnastic. And they say that politics co-operate with nature, but in a less degree, and have more of art; also that legislation is entirely a work of art, and is based on assumptions which are not true.

Cle. How do you mean?

Ath. In the first place, my dear friend, these people would say that the Gods exist not by nature, but by art, and by the laws of states, which are different in different places, according to the agreement of those who make them; and that the honorable is one thing by nature and another thing by law, and that the principles of justice have no existence at all in nature, but that mankind are always disputing about them and altering them; and that the alterations which are made by art and by law have no basis in nature, but are of authority for the moment and at the time at which they are made. — These, my friends, are the sayings of wise men, poets and prose writers, which find a way into the minds of youth. They are told by them that the highest right is might, and in this way the young fall into impieties, under the idea that the Gods are not such as the law bids them imagine; and hence arise factions, these philosophers inviting them to lead a true life according to nature, that is, to live in real dominion over others, and not in legal subjection to them.

Cle. What a dreadful picture, Stranger, have you given, and how great is the injury which is thus inflicted on young men to the ruin both of states and families!

Ath. True, Cleinias; but then what should the lawgiver do when this evil is of long standing? should he only rise up in the state and threaten all mankind, proclaiming that if they will not say and think that the Gods are such as the law ordains (and this may be extended generally to the honorable, the just, and to all the highest things, and to all that relates to virtue and vice), and if they will not make their actions conform to the copy which the law gives them, then he who refuses to obey the law shall die, or suffer stripes and bonds, or privation of citizenship, or in some cases be punished by loss of property and exile? Should he not rather, when he is making laws for men, at the same time infuse the spirit of persuasion into his words, and mitigate the severity of them as far as he can?

Cle. Why, Stranger, if such persuasion be at all possible, then a legislator who has anything in him ought never to weary of persuading men; he ought to leave nothing unsaid in support of the ancient opinion that there are Gods, and of all those other truths which you were just now mentioning; he ought to support the law and also art, and acknowledge that both alike exist by nature, and no less than nature, if they are the creations of mind in accordance with right reason, as you appear to me to maintain, and I am disposed to agree with you in thinking.

Ath. Yes, my enthusiastic Cleinias; but are not these things when spoken to a multitude hard to be understood, not to mention that they take up a dismal length of time?

Cle. Why, Stranger, shall we, whose patience failed not when drinking or music were the themes of discourse, weary now of discoursing about the Gods, and about divine things? And the greatest help to rational legislation is that the laws when once written down are always at rest; they can be put to the test at any future time, and therefore, if on first hearing they seem difficult, there is no reason for apprehension about them, because any man however dull can go over them and consider them again and again; nor if they are tedious but useful, is there any reason or religion, as it seems to me, in any man refusing to maintain the principles of them to the utmost of his power.

Megillus. Stranger, I like what Cleinias is saying.

Ath. Yes, Megillus, and we should do as he proposes; for if impious discourses were not scattered, as I may say, throughout the world, there would have been no need for any vindication of the existence of the Gods — but seeing that they are spread far and wide, such arguments are needed; and who should come to the rescue of the greatest laws, when they are being undermined by bad men, but the legislator himself?

Meg. There is no more proper champion of them.

Ath. Well, then, tell me, Cleinias, — for I must ask you to be my partner, — does not he who talks in this way conceive fire and water and earth and air to be the first elements of all things? these he calls nature, and out of these he supposes the soul to be formed afterwards; and this is not a mere conjecture of ours about his meaning, but is what he really means.

Cle. Very true.

Ath. Then, by Heaven, we have discovered the source of this vain opinion of all those physical investigators; and I would have you examine their arguments with the utmost care, for their impiety is a very serious matter; they not only make a bad and mistaken use of argument, but they lead away the minds of others: that is my opinion of them.

Cle. You are right; but I should like to know how this happens.

Ath. I fear that the argument may seem singular.

Cle. Do not hesitate, Stranger; I see that you are afraid of such a discussion carrying you beyond the limits of legislation. But if there be no other way of showing our agreement in the belief that there are Gods, of whom the law is said now to approve, let us take this way, my good sir.

Ath. Then I suppose that I must repeat the singular argument of those who manufacture the soul according to their own impious notions; they affirm that which is the first cause of the generation and destruction of all things, to be not first, but last, and that which is last to be first, and hence they have fallen into error about the true nature of the Gods.

Cle. Still I do not understand you.

Ath. Nearly all of them, my friends, seem to be ignorant of the nature and power of the soul, especially in what relates to her origin: they do not know that she is among the first of things, and before all bodies, and is the chief author of their changes and transpositions. And if this is true, and if the soul is older than the body, must not the things which are of the soul's kindred be of necessity prior to those which appertain to the body?

Cle. Certainly.

Ath. Then thought and attention and mind and art and law will be prior to that which is hard and soft and heavy and light; and the great and primitive works and actions will be works of art; they will be the first, and after them will come nature and works of nature, which however is a wrong term for men to apply to them; these will follow, and will be under the government of art and mind.

Cle. But why is the word 'nature' wrong?

Ath. Because those who use the term mean to say that nature is the first creative power; but if the soul turn out to be the primeval element, and not fire or air, then in the truest sense and beyond other things the soul may be said to exist by nature; and this would be true if you proved that the soul is older than the body, but not otherwise.

Cle. You are quite right.

Ath. Shall we, then, take this as the next point to which our attention should be directed?

Cle. By all means.

Ath. Let us be on our guard lest this most deceptive argument with its youthful looks, beguiling us old men, give us the slip and make a laughing-stock of us. Who knows but we may be aiming at the greater, and fail to attain the lesser? Suppose that we three have to pass a rapid river, and I, being the youngest of the three and experienced in rivers, take upon me the duty of making the attempt first by myself; leaving you in safety on the bank, I am to examine whether the river is passable by older men like yourselves, and if such appears to be the case then I shall invite you to follow, and my experience will help to convey you across; but if the river is impassable by you, then there will have been no danger to anybody but myself, — would not that seem to be a very fair proposal? I mean to say that the argument in prospect is likely to be too much for you, out of your depth and beyond your strength, and I should be afraid that the stream of my questions might create in you who are not in the habit of answering, giddiness and confusion of mind, and hence a feeling of unpleasantness and unsuitableness might arise. I think therefore that I had better first ask the questions and then answer them myself while you listen in safety; in that way I can carry on the argument until I have completed the proof that the soul is prior to the body.

Cle. Excellent, Stranger, and I hope that you will do as you propose.

Ath. Come, then, and if ever we are to call upon the Gods, let us call upon them now in all seriousness to come to the demonstration of their own existence. And so holding fast to the rope we will venture upon the depths of the argument. When questions of this sort are asked of me, my safest answer would appear to be as follows: — Some one says to me, 'O Stranger, are all things at rest and nothing in motion, or is the exact opposite of this true, or are some things in motion and others at rest?' — To this I shall reply that some things are in motion and others at rest. 'And do not things which move move in a place, and are not the things which are at rest at rest in a place?' Certainly. 'And some move or rest in one place and some in more places than one?' You mean to say, we shall rejoin, that those things which rest at the center move in one place, just as the circumference goes round of globes which are said to be at rest? 'Yes.' And we observe that, in the revolution, the motion which carries round the larger and the lesser circle at the same time is proportionally distributed to greater and smaller, and is greater and smaller in a certain proportion. Here is a wonder which might be thought an impossibility, that the same motion should impart swiftness and slowness in due proportion to larger and lesser circles. 'Very true.' And when you speak of bodies moving in many places, you seem to me to mean those which move from one place to another, and sometimes have one center of motion and sometimes more than one because they turn upon their axis; and whenever they meet anything, if it be stationary, they are divided by it; but if they get in the midst between bodies which are approaching and moving towards the same spot from opposite directions, they unite with them. 'I admit the truth of what you are saying.' Also when they unite they grow, and when they are divided they waste away, — that is, supposing the constitution of each to remain, or if that fails, then there is a second reason of their dissolution. 'And when are all things created and how?' Clearly, they are created when the first principle receives increase and attains to the second dimension, and from this arrives at the one which is neighbor to this, and after reaching the third becomes perceptible to sense. Everything which is thus changing and moving is in process of generation; only when at rest has it real existence, but when passing into another state it is destroyed utterly. Have we not mentioned all motions that there are, and comprehended them under their kinds and numbered them with the exception, my friends, of two?

Cle. Which are they?

Ath. Just the two, with which our present enquiry is concerned.

Cle. Speak plainer.

Ath. I suppose that our enquiry has reference to the soul?

Cle. Very true.

Ath. Let us assume that there is a motion able to move other things, but not to move itself; — that is one kind; and there is another kind which can move itself as well as other things, working in composition and decomposition, by increase and diminution and generation and destruction, — that is also one of the many kinds of motion.

Cle. Granted.

Ath. And we will assume that which moves other, and is changed by other, to be the ninth, and that which changes itself and others, and is co-incident with every action and every passion, and is the true principle of change and motion in all that is, — that we shall be inclined to call the tenth.

Cle. Certainly.

Ath. And which of these ten motions ought we to prefer as being the mightiest and most efficient?

Cle. I must say that the motion which is able to move itself is ten thousand times superior to all the others.

Ath. Very good; but may I make one or two corrections in what I have been saying?

Cle. What are they?

Ath. When I spoke of the tenth sort of motion, that was not quite correct.

Cle. What was the error?

Ath. According to the true order, the tenth was really the first in generation and power; then follows the second, which was strangely enough termed the ninth by us.

Cle. What do you mean?

Ath. I mean this: when one thing changes another, and that another, of such will there be any primary changing element? How can a thing which is moved by another ever be the beginning of change? Impossible. But when the self-moved changes other, and that again other, and thus thousands upon tens of thousands of bodies are set in motion, must not the beginning of all this motion be the change of the self-moving principle?

Cle. Very true, and I quite agree.

Ath. Or, to put the question in another way, making answer to ourselves: — If, as most of these philosophers have the audacity to affirm, all things were at rest in one mass, which of the above-mentioned principles of motion would first spring up among them?

Cle. Clearly the self-moving; for there could be no change in them arising out of any external cause; the change must first take place in themselves.

Ath. Then we must say that self-motion being the origin of all motions, and the first which arises among things at rest as well as among things in motion, is the eldest and mightiest principle of change, and that which is changed by another and yet moves other is second.

Cle. Quite true.

Ath. At this stage of the argument let us put a question.

Cle. What question?

Ath. If we were to see this power existing in any earthy, watery, or fiery substance, simple or compound — how should we describe it?

Cle. You mean to ask whether we should call such a self-moving power life?

Ath. I do.

Cle. Certainly we should.

Ath. And when we see soul in anything, must we not do the same — must we not admit that this is life?

Cle. We must.

Ath. And now, I beseech you, reflect; — you would admit that we have a threefold knowledge of things?

Cle. What do you mean?

Ath. I mean that we know the essence, and that we know the definition of the essence, and the name, — these are the three; and there are two questions which may be raised about anything.

Cle. How two?

Ath. Sometimes a person may give the name and ask the definition; or he may give the definition and ask the name. I may illustrate what I mean in this way.

Cle. How?

Ath. Number like some other things is capable of being divided into equal parts; when thus divided, number is named

' even,' and the definition of the name ' even ' is ' number divisible into two equal parts '?

Cle. True.

Ath. I mean, that when we are asked about the definition and give the name, or when we are asked about the name and give the definition — in either case, whether we give name or definition, we speak of the same thing, calling ' even ' the number which is divided into two equal parts.

Cle. Quite true.

Ath. And what is the definition of that which is named ' soul '? Can we conceive of any other than that which has been already given — the motion which can move itself?

Cle. You mean to say that the essence which is defined as the self-moved is the same with that which has the name soul?

Ath. Yes; and if this is true, do we still maintain that there is anything wanting in the proof that the soul is the first origin and moving power of all that is, or has become, or will be, and their contraries, when she has been clearly shown to be the source of change and motion in all things?

Cle. Certainly not; the soul as being the source of motion, has been most satisfactorily shown to be the oldest of all things.

Ath. And is not that motion which is produced in another, by reason of another, but never has any self-moving power at all, being in truth the change of an inanimate body, to be reckoned second, or by any lower number which you may prefer?

Cle. Exactly.

Ath. Then we are right, and speak the most perfect and absolute truth, when we say that the soul is prior to the body, and that the body is second and comes afterwards, and is born to obey the soul, which is the ruler?

Cle. Nothing can be more true.

Ath. Do you remember our old admission, that if the soul was prior to the body the things of the soul were also prior to those of the body?

Cle. Certainly.

Ath. Then characters and manners, and wishes and reasonings, and true opinions, and reflections, and recollections are prior to length and breadth and depth and strength of bodies, if the soul is prior to the body.

Cle. To be sure.

Ath. In the next place, must we not of necessity admit that the soul is the cause of good and evil, base and honorable, just and unjust, and of all other opposites, if we suppose her to be the cause of all things?

Cle. We must.

Ath. And as the soul orders and inhabits all things that move, however moving, must we not say that she orders also the heavens?

Cle. Of course.

Ath. One soul or more? More than one — I will answer for you; at any rate, we must not suppose that there are less than two — one the author of good, and the other of evil.

Cle. Very true.

Ath. Yes, very true; the soul then directs all things in heaven, and earth, and sea by her movements, and these are described by the terms — will, consideration, attention, deliberation, opinion true and false, joy and sorrow, confidence, fear, hatred, love, and other primary motions akin to these; which again receive the secondary motions of corporeal substances, and guide all things to growth and decay, to composition and decomposition, and to the qualities which accompany them, such as heat and cold, heaviness and lightness, hardness and softness, blackness and whiteness, bitterness and sweetness, and all those other qualities which the soul uses, herself a goddess, when truly receiving the divine mind she disciplines all things rightly to their happiness; but when she is the companion of folly, she does the very contrary of all this. Shall we assume so much, or do we still entertain doubts?

Cle. There is no room at all for doubt.

(Vol. II, pp. 628–39)

Selections from Aristotle*

FROM THE *PHYSICS*, BOOK II, CHAPTER I

[The *Physics* is devoted to a study of "the number and character of the first principles of nature." This particular section deals with "nature and the natural." It introduces us to the sage's relentless determination to proceed by means of careful description and precise definition. Not easy reading, to be sure, but most rewarding to one who persists with patience.]

Of things that exist, some exist by nature, some from other causes. 'By nature' the animals and their parts exist, and the plants and the simple bodies (earth, fire, air, water) — for we say that these and the like exist 'by nature.'

All the things mentioned present a feature in which they differ from things which are *not* constituted by nature. Each of them has *within itself* a principle of motion and of stationariness (in respect of place, or of growth and decrease, or by way of alteration). On the other hand, a bed and a coat and anything else of that sort, *qua* receiving these designations — i.e. in so far as they are products of art — have no innate impulse to change. But in so far as they happen to be composed of stone or of earth or of a mixture of the two, they *do* have such an impulse, and just to that extent — which seems to indicate that *nature is a source or cause of being moved and of being at rest in that to which it belongs primarily,* in virtue of itself and not in virtue of a concomitant attribute.

I say 'not in virtue of a concomitant attribute,' because (for instance) a man who is a doctor might cure himself. Nevertheless it is not in so far as he is a patient that he possesses the art

---

* These selections are taken from *The Basic Works of Aristotle,* edited by Richard McKeon (New York: Random House, 1941). McKeon's selections are taken from *The Works of Aristotle,* translated and edited by W. D. Ross. Copyright Oxford University Press.

of medicine: it merely has happened that the same man is doctor and patient — and that is why these attributes are not always found together. So it is with all other artificial products. None of them has in itself the source of its own production. But while in some cases (for instance houses and the other products of manual labour) that principle is in something else external to the thing, in others — those which may cause a change in themselves in virtue of a concomitant attribute — it lies in the things themselves (but not in virtue of what they are).

'Nature' then is what has been stated. Things 'have a nature' which have a principle of this kind. Each of them is a substance; for it is a subject, and nature always implies a subject in which it inheres.

The term 'according to nature' is applied to all these things and also to the attributes which belong to them in virtue of what they are, for instance the property of fire to be carried upwards — which is not a 'nature' nor 'has a nature' but is 'by nature' or 'according to nature.'

What nature is, then, and the meaning of the terms 'by nature' and 'according to nature,' has been stated. *That* nature exists, it would be absurd to try to prove; for it is obvious that there are many things of this kind, and to prove what is obvious by what is not is the mark of a man who is unable to distinguish what is self-evident from what is not. (This state of mind is clearly possible. A man blind from birth might reason about colours. Presumably therefore such persons must be talking about words without any thought to correspond.)

Some identify the nature or substance of a natural object with that immediate constituent of it which taken by itself is without arrangement, e.g. the wood is the 'nature' of the bed, and the bronze the 'nature' of the statue.

As an indication of this Antiphon points out that if you planted a bed and the rotting wood acquired the power of sending up a shoot, it would not be a bed that would come up, but *wood* — which shows that the arrangement in accordance with the rules of the art is merely an incidental attribute, whereas the real nature is the other, which, further, persists continuously through the process of making.

But if the material of each of these objects has itself the same relation to something else, say bronze (or gold) to water, bones (or wood) to earth and so on, *that* (they say) would be their nature and essence. Consequently some assert earth, others fire or air or water or some or all of these, to be the nature of the things that are. For whatever any one of them supposed to have this character — whether one thing or more than one thing — this or these he declared to be the whole of substance, all else being its affections, states, or dispositions. Every such thing they held to be eternal (for it could not pass into anything else), but other things to come into being and cease to be times without number.

This then is one account of ' nature,' namely that it is the immediate material substratum of things which have in themselves a principle of motion or change.

Another account is that ' nature ' is the shape or form which is specified in the definition of the thing.

For the word ' nature ' is applied to what is according to nature and the natural in the same way as ' art ' is applied to what is artistic or a work of art. We should not say in the latter case that there is anything artistic about a thing, if it is a bed only potentially, not yet having the form of a bed; nor should we call it a work of art. The same is true of natural compounds. What is potentially flesh or bone has not yet its own ' nature,' and does not exist ' by nature,' until it receives the form specified in the definition, which we name in defining what flesh or bone is. Thus in the second sense of ' nature ' it would be the shape or form (not separable except in statement) of things which have in themselves a source of motion. (The combination of the two, e.g. man, is not ' nature ' but ' by nature ' or ' natural.')

The form indeed is ' nature ' rather than the matter; for a thing is more properly said to be what it is when it has attained to fulfilment than when it exists potentially. Again man is born from man, but not bed from bed. That is why people say that the figure is not the nature of a bed, but the wood is — if the bed sprouted not a bed but wood would come up. But even if the figure *is* art, then on the same principle the shape of man is his nature. For man is born from man.

We also speak of a thing's nature as being exhibited in the process of growth by which its nature is attained. The ' nature ' in this sense is not like ' doctoring,' which leads not to the art of doctoring but to health. Doctoring must start from the art, not lead to it. But it is not in this way that nature (in the one sense) is related to nature (in the other). What grows *qua* growing grows from something into something. Into what then does it grow? Not into that from which it arose but into that to which it tends. The shape then is nature.

'Shape' and 'nature,' it should be added, are used in two senses. For the privation too is in a way form. But whether in unqualified coming to be there is privation, i.e. a contrary to what comes to be, we must consider later. (*Pp. 236–38*)

FROM THE *PHYSICS*, BOOK VIII, CHAPTER I

[Preceding sections of the treatise have brought up, at this point, the problem of the meaning of motion. How shall it be regarded? Is it the basic category in terms of which all being can be explained? These short excerpts are included because they illustrate the sweep of Aristotle's approach to a question. The concluding excerpt demonstrates the vigor with which he clinches an argument.]

It remains to consider the following question. Was there ever a becoming of motion before which it had no being, and is it perishing again so as to leave nothing in motion? Or are we to say that it never had any becoming and is not perishing, but always was and always will be? Is it in fact an immortal never-failing property of things that are, a sort of life as it were to all naturally constituted things?

Now the *existence* of motion is asserted by all who have anything to say about nature, because they all concern themselves with the construction of the world and study the question of becoming and perishing, which processes could not come about without the existence of motion. But those who say that there is an infinite number of worlds, some of which are in process of becoming while others are in process of perishing, assert that there is always motion (for these processes of becoming and perishing of the worlds necessarily involve motion), whereas those who hold that there is only one world, whether everlasting or not, make corresponding assumptions in regard to motion. If then it is possible that at any time nothing should be in motion, this must come about in one of two ways: either in the manner described by Anaxagoras, who says that all things were together and at rest for an infinite period of time, and that then Mind introduced motion and separated them; or in the manner described by Empedocles, according to whom the universe is alternately in motion and at rest — in motion, when Love is making the one out of many, or

Strife is making many out of one, and at rest in the intermediate periods of time — his account being as follows:

> ' Since One hath learned to spring from Manifold,
> And One disjoined makes Manifold arise,
> Thus they Become, nor stable is their life:
> But since their motion must alternate be,
> Thus have they ever Rest upon their round ':

for we must suppose that he means by this that they alternate from the one motion to the other. We must consider, then, how this matter stands, for the discovery of the truth about it is of importance, not only for the study of nature, but also for the investigation of the First Principle.

Resuming our main argument, we proceed from the positions that there must be continuous motion in the world of things, that this is a single motion, that a single motion must be a motion of a magnitude (for that which is without magnitude cannot be in motion), and that the magnitude must be a single magnitude moved by a single movent (for otherwise there will not be continuous motion but a consecutive series of separate motions), and that if the movent is a single thing, it is either itself in motion or itself unmoved: if, then, it is in motion, it will have to be subject to the same conditions as that which it moves, that is to say it will itself be in process of change and in being so will also have to be moved by something: so we have a series that must come to an end, and a point will be reached at which motion is imparted by something that is unmoved. Thus we have a movent that has no need to change along with that which it moves but will be able to cause motion always (for the causing of motion under these conditions involves no effort): and this motion alone is regular, or at least it is so in a higher degree than any other, since the movent is never subject to any change. So, too, in order that the motion may continue to be of the same character, the moved must not be subject to change in respect of its relation to the movent. Moreover the movent must occupy either the centre or the circumference, since these are the first principles from which a sphere is derived. But the things nearest the movent are those whose motion is quickest, and in this case it is the motion of the circumference that is the quickest: therefore the movent occupies the circumference.

There is a further difficulty in supposing it to be possible for anything that is in motion to cause motion continuously and not merely in the way in which it is caused by something repeatedly pushing (in which case the continuity amounts to no more than successiveness). Such a movent must either itself continue to push or pull or perform both these actions, or else the action must be taken up by something else and be passed on from one movent to another (the process that we described before as occurring in the case of things thrown, since the air or the water, being divisible, is a movent only in virtue of the fact that different parts of the air are moved one after another): and in either case the motion cannot be a single motion, but only a consecutive series of motions. The only continuous motion, then, is that which is caused by the unmoved movent: and this motion is continuous because the movent remains always invariable, so that its relation to that which it moves remains also invariable and continuous.

Now that these points are settled, it is clear that the first unmoved movent cannot have any magnitude. For if it has magnitude, this must be either a finite or an infinite magnitude. Now we have already proved in our course on Physics that there cannot be an infinite magnitude: and we have now proved that it is impossible for a finite magnitude to have an infinite force, and also that it is impossible for a thing to be moved by a finite magnitude during an infinite time. But the first movent causes a motion that is eternal and does cause it during an infinite time. It is clear, therefore, that the first movent is indivisible and is without parts and without magnitude. (*Pp. 354–55; 393–94*)

FROM *ON THE SOUL,* BOOK II, CHAPTER I

[Aristotle is here trying to solve the puzzle of what the soul is and how it is related to the body. Thomas Aquinas made this line of reasoning do yeoman service in Christian theology.]

Let the foregoing suffice as our account of the views concerning the soul which have been handed on by our predecessors; let us now dismiss them and make as it were a completely fresh start, endeavouring to give a precise answer to the question, What is soul? i.e. to formulate the most general possible definition of it.

We are in the habit of recognizing, as one determinate kind of what is, substance, and that in several senses, (*a*) in the sense of matter or that which in itself is not 'a this,' and (*b*) in the sense of form or essence, which is that precisely in virtue of which a thing is called 'a this,' and thirdly (*c*) in the sense of that which is compounded of both (*a*) and (*b*). Now matter is potentiality, form actuality; of the latter there are two grades related to one another as e.g. knowledge to the exercise of knowledge.

Among substances are by general consent reckoned bodies and especially natural bodies; for they are the principles of all other bodies. Of natural bodies some have life in them, others not; by life we mean self-nutrition and growth (with its correlative decay). It follows that every natural body which has life in it is a substance in the sense of a composite.

But since it is also a *body* of such and such a kind, viz. having life, the *body* cannot be soul; the body is the subject or matter, not what is attributed to it. Hence the soul must be a substance in the sense of the form of a natural body having life potentially within it. But substance is actuality, and thus soul is the actuality of a body as above characterized. Now the word actuality has two senses corresponding respectively to the possession of knowledge and the actual exercise of knowledge. It is obvious that the soul is actuality in the first sense, viz. that of knowledge as possessed, for both sleeping and waking presuppose the existence of soul, and of these waking corresponds to actual knowing, sleeping to knowledge possessed but not employed, and, in the history of the individual, knowledge comes before its employment or exercise.

That is why the soul is the first grade of actuality of a natural body having life potentially in it. The body so described is a body which is organized. The parts of plants in spite of their extreme simplicity are ' organs '; e.g. the leaf serves to shelter the pericarp, the pericarp to shelter the fruit, while the roots of plants are analogous to the mouth of animals, both serving for the absorption of food. If, then, we have to give a general formula applicable to all kinds of soul, we must describe it as the first grade of actuality of a natural organized body. That is why we can wholly dismiss as unnecessary the question whether the soul and the body are one: it is as meaningless as to ask whether the wax and the shape given to it by the stamp are one, or generally the matter of a thing and that of which it is the matter. Unity has many senses (as many as ' is ' has), but the most proper and fundamental sense of both is the relation of an actuality to that of which it is the actuality.

We have now given an answer to the question, What is soul? — an answer which applies to it in its full extent. It is substance in the sense which corresponds to the definitive formula of a thing's essence. That means that it is ' the essential whatness ' of a body of the character just assigned. Suppose that what is literally an ' organ,' like an axe, were a *natural* body, its ' essential whatness,' would have been its essence, and so its soul; if this disappeared from it, it would have ceased to be an axe, except in name. As it is, it is just an axe; it wants the character which is required to make its whatness or formulable essence a soul; for that, it would have had to be a *natural* body of a particular kind, viz. one having *in itself* the power of setting itself in movement and arresting itself. Next, apply this doctrine in the case of the ' parts ' of the living body. Suppose that the eye were an animal — sight would have been its soul, for sight is the substance or essence of the eye which corresponds to the formula, the eye being merely the matter of seeing; when seeing is removed the eye is no longer an eye, except in name — it is no more a real eye than the eye of a statue or of a painted figure. We must now extend our consideration from the ' parts ' to the whole living body; for what the departmental sense is to the bodily part which is its organ, that the whole faculty of sense is to the whole sensitive body as such.

We must not understand by that which is 'potentially capable of living' what has lost the soul it had, but only what still retains it; but seeds and fruits are bodies which possess the qualification. Consequently, while waking is actuality in the sense corresponding to the cutting and the seeing, the soul is actuality in the sense corresponding to the power of sight and the power in the tool; the body corresponds to what exists in potentiality; as the pupil *plus* the power of sight constitutes the eye, so the soul *plus* the body constitutes the animal.

From this it indubitably follows that the soul is inseparable from its body, or at any rate that certain parts of it are (if it has parts) — for the actuality of some of them is nothing but the actualities of their bodily parts. Yet some may be separable because they are not the actualities of any body at all. Further, we have no light on the problem whether the soul may not be the actuality of its body in the sense in which the sailor is the actuality of the ship.

This must suffice as our sketch or outline determination of the nature of the soul. (*Pp. 554–56*)

FROM THE *NICHOMACHEAN ETHICS*,
BOOK X, CHAPTER VIII

[Aristotle's ethics and theology, like Plato's, frequently flow together. In the following passage something like this has occurred. The highest activity of man is akin to the continuous activity of God, and when man is " likest God " he enjoys " perfect happiness."]

But that perfect happiness is a contemplative activity will appear from the following consideration as well. We assume the gods to be above all other beings blessed and happy; but what sort of actions must we assign to them? Acts of justice? Will not the gods seem absurd if they make contracts and return deposits, and so on? Acts of a brave man, then, confronting dangers and running risks because it is noble to do so? Or liberal acts? To whom will they give? It will be strange if they are really to have money or anything of the kind. And what would their temperate acts be? Is not such praise tasteless, since they have no bad appetites? If we were to run through them all, the circumstances of action would be found trivial and unworthy of gods. Still, every one supposes that they *live* and therefore that they are active; we cannot suppose them to sleep like Endymion. Now if you take away from a living being action, and still more production, what is left but contemplation? Therefore the activity of God, which surpasses all others in blessedness, must be contemplative; and of human activities, therefore, that which is most akin to this must be most of the nature of happiness.

This is indicated, too, by the fact that the other animals have no share in happiness, being completely deprived of such activity. For while the whole life of the gods is blessed, and that of men too in so far as some likeness of such activity belongs to them, none of the other animals is happy, since they in no way share in contemplation. Happiness extends, then, just so far as contemplation does, and those to whom contemplation more fully belongs are more truly happy, not as a mere concomitant but in virtue of the contemplation; for this is in itself precious. Happiness, therefore, must be some form of contemplation.

But, being a man, one will also need external prosperity; for our nature is not self-sufficient for the purpose of contemplation, but our body also must be healthy and must have food and other attention. Still, we must not think that the man who is to be happy will need many things or great things, merely because he cannot be supremely happy without external goods; for self-sufficiency and action do not involve excess, and we can do noble acts without ruling earth and sea; for even with moderate advantages one can act virtuously (this is manifest enough; for private persons are thought to do worthy acts no less than despots — indeed even more); and it is enough that we should have so much as that; for the life of the man who is active in accordance with virtue will be happy. Solon, too, was perhaps sketching well the happy man when he described him as moderately furnished with externals but as having done (as Solon thought) the noblest acts, and lived temperately; for one can with but moderate possessions do what one ought. Anaxagoras also seems to have supposed the happy man not to be rich nor a despot, when he said that he would not be surprised if the happy man were to seem to most people a strange person; for they judge by externals, since these are all they perceive. The opinions of the wise seem, then, to harmonize with our arguments. But while even such things carry some conviction, the truth in practical matters is discerned from the facts of life; for these are the decisive factor. We must therefore survey what we have already said, bringing it to the test of the facts of life, and if it harmonizes with the facts we must accept it, but if it clashes with them we must suppose it to be mere theory. Now he who exercises his reason and cultivates it seems to be both in the best state of mind and most dear to the gods. For if the gods have any care for human affairs, as they are thought to have, it would be reasonable both that they should delight in that which was best and most akin to them (i.e. reason) and that they should reward those who love and honour this most, as caring for the things that are dear to them and acting both rightly and nobly. And that all these attributes belong most of all to the philosopher is manifest. He, therefore, is the dearest to the gods. And he who is that will presumably be also the happiest; so that in this way too the philosopher will more than any other be happy.

(*Pp. 1106–8*)

FROM THE *METAPHYSICS*, BOOK VI, CHAPTER I

[In this section of the treatise, Aristotle is pressing the inquiry regarding the different kinds of causes. He finds three general categories of causation, and designates the science to deal with each one. Theology, to him, is as natural a science as mathematics and physics. What is more, she is the "Queen of the Sciences" to him.]

We are seeking the principles and the causes of the things that are, and obviously of them *qua* being. For, while there is a cause of health and of good condition, and the objects of mathematics have first principles and elements and causes, and in general every science which is ratiocinative or at all involves reasoning deals with causes and principles, more or less precise, all these sciences mark off some particular being — some genus, and inquire into this, but not into being simply nor *qua* being, nor do they offer any discussion of the essence of the things of which they treat; but starting from the essence — some making it plain to the senses, others assuming it as a hypothesis — they then demonstrate, more or less cogently, the essential attributes of the genus with which they deal. It is obvious, therefore, that such an induction yields no demonstration of substance or of the essence, but some other way of exhibiting it. And similarly the sciences omit the question whether the genus with which they deal exists or does not exist, because it belongs to the same kind of thinking to show what it is and that it is.

And since natural science, like other sciences, is in fact about one class of being, i.e. to that sort of substance which has the principle of its movement and rest present in itself, evidently it is neither practical nor productive. For in the case of things made the principle is in the maker — it is either reason or art or some faculty, while in the case of things done it is in the doer — viz. will, for that which is done and that which is willed are the same. Therefore, if all thought is either practical or productive or theoretical, physics must be a theoretical science, but it will theorize

156

about such being as admits of being moved, and about substance-as-defined for the most part only as not separable from matter. Now, we must not fail to notice the mode of being of the essence and of its definition, for, without this, inquiry is but idle. Of things defined, i.e. of 'whats,' some are like ' snub,' and some like ' concave.' And these differ because 'snub' is bound up with matter (for what is snub is a concave *nose*), while concavity is independent of perceptible matter. If then all natural things are analogous to the snub in their nature — e.g. nose, eye, face, flesh, bone, and, in general, animal; leaf, root, bark, and, in general, plant (for none of these can be defined without reference to movement — they always have matter), it is clear how we must seek and define the 'what' in the case of natural objects, and also that it belongs to the student of nature to study even soul in a certain sense, i.e. so much of it as is not independent of matter.

That physics, then, is a theoretical science, is plain from these considerations. Mathematics also, however, is theoretical; but whether its objects are immovable and separable from matter, is not at present clear; still, it is clear that *some* mathematical theorems *consider* them *qua* immovable and *qua* separable from matter. But if there is something which is eternal and immovable and separable, clearly the knowledge of it belongs to a theoretical science — not, however, to physics (for physics deals with certain movable things) nor to mathematics, but to a science prior to both. For physics deals with things which exist separately but are not immovable, and some parts of mathematics deal with things which are immovable but presumably do not exist separately, but as embodied in matter; while the first science deals with things which both exist separately and are immovable. Now all causes must be eternal, but especially these; for they are the causes that operate on so much of the divine as appears to us. There must, then, be three theoretical philosophies, mathematics, physics, and what we may call theology, since it is obvious that if the divine is present anywhere, it is present in things of this sort. And the highest science must deal with the highest genus. Thus, while the theoretical sciences are more to be desired than the other sciences, this is more to be desired than the other theoretical sciences. For one might raise the question whether first philosophy is universal, or deals with one genus, i.e. some one kind of being; for not even the mathematical sciences are all alike in this respect — geometry and astronomy deal with a certain particular kind of thing, while universal mathematics applies alike to all. We answer that if there is no substance other than those which are formed by nature, natural science will be the first science; but if there is an immovable substance, the science of this must be prior and must be first philosophy, and universal in this way, because it is first. And it will belong to this to consider being *qua* being — both what it is and the attributes which belong to it *qua* being.   (*Pp.* 778–79)

Selections from Plotinus *

"THE NATURE AND SOURCE OF EVIL"

[The following discussion of the character of evil was a powerful formative factor in Augustine's theology, and through him in the thought of the Christian church on this eternal theme.]

Let us define the nature of the Good as far as our immediate purpose demands.

The Good is that on which all depends, towards which all existences aspire as to their source and need, while Itself is without need, the measure and term of all, giving out from Itself Divine Mind and Being and Soul and Life and all intellective act.

The Good is beyond beautiful, beyond the Highest, holding kingly state in that Intellectual Cosmos of which the Principle is wholly unlike what is known as intelligence in us. Our intelligence works by reasonings, examines links of demonstration, and comes to know the world of Being also by the steps of logical process, having no prior grasp of Reality, but remaining empty, all intelligence though it be, until it has put itself to school.

But the Divine Mind is not of such a kind. It possesses all, It is all. It has all by other means than having, for what It possesses is still Itself.

And the First Act is the Act of the Good stationary within Itself; but there is also an Act directed towards It, that of the Divine Mind which, as it were, lives about It. And Soul circles around Divine Mind and by gazing upon It, seeing into the depths of It, through It sees God.

Such is the untroubled, blissful life of divine Beings, and evil has no place in it.

If evil exist at all, it must be situate in the realm of non-being. By this non-being we are not to understand something that simply

* These selections are taken from *The Essence of Plotinus,* compiled by Grace H. Turnbull (New York: Oxford University Press, 1934).

159

does not exist, but only something of an utterly different order from Authentic Being. Some conception of it would be reached by thinking of measurelessness as opposed to measure, the unshaped against a shaping principle, the ever-needy against the self-sufficing; while whatever participates in it and resembles it becomes evil, though not to the point of being evil absolute.

What then is the evil soul?

It is the soul that accepts unmeasure, excess and shortcoming which bring forth licentiousness, cowardice and all other flaws of the soul, all the states, foreign to the true nature, which set up false judgments, so that the soul comes to name evil or good those things which it respectively flees or pursues (rather than to test them by their true value). Such a soul is not purely itself; it is shut out from the Forming Idea that orders and brings to measure, and this because it is merged in a body made of matter.

Then if the reasoning faculty too has taken hurt, the soul's seeing is balked by the passions and by the darkening that matter brings to it, by its attention no longer to essence but to process whose principle or source is matter. Wholly without part in Good, the negation of Good, unmingled lack, this matter-kind makes over to its own likeness whatsoever comes in touch with it.

But the soul wrought to perfection, addressed towards Divine Mind, is stedfastly pure; it has turned away from matter; all that is undetermined, that is outside of measure, that is evil, it neither sees nor draws near; it endures in its purity wholly determined by Divine Mind.

How do we explain the teaching that evils can never pass away but exist of necessity; that while evil has no place in the divine order, it haunts mortal nature and this place forever? Does this mean that heaven is clear of evil, ever moving its orderly way, spinning on the appointed path, no injustice there nor any flaw, no wrong done by any power to any other, while injustice and disorder prevail on earth?

Not quite so; for the precept to " flee hence " does not refer to earth and earthly life. The flight consists not in quitting earth but in living our earth-life with justice and piety in the light of philosophy; it is vice we are to flee. The escape is not a matter of place, but of acquiring virtue, of disengaging the self from the body; this is the escape from matter. The soul's " separate place " is simply its not being in matter, not being united with it, not molded in matter as in a matrix. This is the soul's apartness.

Given that the Good is not the only existent thing, it is inevitable that by the outgoing from It, the continuous down-going from It, there should be produced a last; this will be evil. This last, the thing which has no residue of Good in it, is matter.

Matter becomes mistress of what is manifested through it; it corrupts and destroys the incomer, it substitutes its own opposite character and kind by setting its excess and defect against the duly ordered. Thus what enters into matter ceases to belong to itself, comes to belong to matter, just as in the nourishment of living beings what is taken in does not remain as it came, but is turned into blood and becomes in fact any of the humors of the recipient. If, then, body is the cause of evil, there is no escape; the cause of evil is matter.

But how may we know good and evil?

Virtue we may know by Divine Mind and by means of the philosophic habit; but vice?

As a ruler marks off straight from crooked, so vice is known by its divergence from the line of virtue.

Virtue is not the absolute Good and Beauty, because we know that these are earlier than virtue and transcend it, and that it is good and beautiful by some participation in them. Now as going upward from virtue we come to the Beautiful and Good, so, going downward from vice, we reach essential evil. We are become dwellers in the place of unlikeness, where, fallen from all our resemblance to the Divine, we lie in gloom and mud; for if the soul abandons itself unreservedly to the extreme of viciousness, as far as soul can die it is dead. This is our " going down to Hades and slumbering there."

The vicious soul is unstable, swept along from every ill to every other, quickly stirred by appetites, headlong to anger, as hasty to compromises, yielding at once to obscure imaginations; as weak, in fact, as the weakest thing made by man or nature, blown about by every breeze and eddy.

But the faculties of the soul are many, and it has its beginning, its intermediate phases, its uttermost border. Matter importunes, raises disorders, seeks to force its way within; but all the ground is holy, nothing there without part in Soul. Matter therefore submits, and takes light; but the source of its illumination it cannot attain to, for the soul cannot endure this foreign thing. On the contrary the illumination streaming from the soul is dulled as it mixes with matter.

This is the fall of the soul, this entry into matter; thence its weakness; not all the faculties of its being retain free play, for matter hinders their manifestation; it encroaches upon the soul's territory and, as it were, crushes the soul back and turns to evil what it has stolen until that finds strength to rise again.

Thus the cause of the weakness of soul and of all its evil is matter. What soul could contain evil unless by contact with the lower kind? There could be no desire, no sorrow, no rage, no fear; fear touches the compounded dreading its dissolution; desires spring from something troubling the grouped being or are a provision against trouble threatened; the soul takes up false notions through having gone outside of its own truth by ceasing to be purely itself.

The appetite or desire for the Divine Mind is something wholly other; with That, then, must the soul unite, dwelling alone enshrined in That, never lapsing towards the less.   (*Pp. 54–58*)

"THE GOOD AND THE ONE"

[Here again Plotinus' penchant for careful definition and an almost tropical richness of description is clearly seen. He outlines no easy method of apprehending the Good, of knowing the One. It begins by a careful study and weighing of the world of sense, and ends with the soul poised for a mystical flight into the area of Being beyond the reach of sense, reflection and reason. Plotinus, like his great master, Plato, could write with warm tenderness and true reverence about God and his works.]

It is in virtue of unity that beings are beings. What could exist at all except as one thing? An army, a choir, a flock, deprived of unity, cease to exist. Health, similarly, is the condition of a body acting as a coordinate unity. Beauty appears when limbs and features are controlled by this principle. Moral excellence is of a soul acting as a concordant total, brought to unity.

Anything that can be described as a unity is so in the precise degree in which it holds a characteristic being; the less or more the degree of the being, the less or more the unity. Soul is a thing of greater unity in proportion as it is of the greater, the authentic being; but absolute unity it is not. Looser aggregates such as a choir are furthest from unity, the more compact are the nearer. Anything losing unity loses its being. Mind, holding itself in the presence of the Good and the First and looking simultaneously upon itself and upon its Transcendent, is manifold, and thus far from being the Unity.

What then must the Unity be? What nature is left for It?

To state it is not easy; the soul reaching towards the formless finds itself incompetent to grasp where nothing bounds it; in sheer dread of holding to nothingness, it grows troubled and often descends from this vagueness to the realm of sense, there to rest as on solid ground: just as the sight, distressed by minute objects, rests with pleasure on the bold. Soul must see in its own way; this is by coalescence, unification; but in seeking thus to know the

163

Unity it is prevented by that very unification from recognizing that it has found; it cannot distinguish itself from the object of this intuition. Nonetheless, this is our one resource if our philosophy is to give us knowledge of the Unity.

We are in search of Unity, the Principle of all, the Good and the First; therefore we may not lie prostrate among the lasts; rising from those things of sense, we must strike for the realm of Firsts. Cleared of all evil in our intention towards the Good, we must ascend to the Principle within ourselves; from many, we must become one. Shaping ourselves into Divine Mind, making over our soul to That and establishing it Therein, what That sees the soul will waken to see. It must be our care to bring over nothing whatever from sense; with Mind pure, and with the summit of Mind, we are to see the All-Pure.

The main difficulty is that awareness of this Principle comes not by knowing but by a presence passing knowledge. In knowing the mind takes account of things; thus plunging into multiplicity, it departs from unity. Our way takes us beyond knowing; in our writing and telling we are but urging towards It; out of discussion we call to vision; to those desiring to see, we point the path; our teaching is a guiding in the way; the seeing must be the very act of him who has made this choice.

There are those that have not attained to see. The soul has not come to know the splendor There; it has not felt and clutched to itself that love-passion of vision known to the lover come to rest where he loves. Or, struck perhaps by that authentic light, all the soul lit by the nearness gained, we have gone weighted from beneath; the vision is frustrate; we should go without burden, and we have gone carrying that which can but keep us back; we are not yet made over into Unity. Present, that Principle yet remains absent from all save those fit to receive, disciplined into some accordance, able to touch It closely by their likeness and by that kindred power within themselves through which, remaining as it was when it came to them from the Supreme, they are enabled to see in so far as God may be seen at all.

That awesome Prior, the Unity, is not a being, for so Its unity would be vested in something else; strictly no name is apt to It, but there is a certain rough fitness in designating It as Unity with the understanding that It is not the unity of some other thing such

as point or monad. Nor is Its impartibility that of extreme minuteness; on the contrary It is great beyond anything, infinite not
in measureless extension or numerable quantity but in fathomless depths of power. It is wholly self-existent. Something there
must be supremely adequate, autonomous, all-transcending, most
utterly without need. All need is effort towards a first principle;
the First, Principle to all, must be without need of anything.

If the mind reels before something thus alien to all we know,
we must take our stand on the things of this realm and strive
thence to see. But in the looking beware of throwing the thought
outward; this Principle does not lie away in some one place leaving the rest void; to those of power to reach, It is present; to the
unapt, absent. In our daily affairs we cannot hold an object in
mind if we are occupied with some other matter; so here, preoccupied by the impress of something else, we are withheld from
becoming aware of the Unity; a mind gripped and fastened by
some definite thing cannot take the print of the very contrary. If
the soul is to be brimmed and lit by the Primal Principle, we must
withdraw it from all the outer, the self put out of mind in the contemplation of the Supreme, all the commerce so closely There
that, if possible, one might bring word to others of that heavenly
intercourse. God is outside of none, present unperceived to all;
we break away from Him, or rather from ourselves; what we turn
from we cannot reach; astray ourselves, we cannot go in search of
another; a child distraught will not recognize its father; but if we
know ourselves we shall also know whence we are.

The natural course of the soul is in a circle round its center,
the point to which it owes its rise. The soul's movement will be
about its Source; to This it will hold, poised intent towards that
Unity to which all souls should move and the divine souls always
move, divine in virtue of that movement; for to be integral with
the Supreme is to be a god; what stands away is multiple still, or
beast.

The soul is not a circle in the sense of a geometric figure but in
that it at once contains the Primal Nature (as center) and is contained by It (as circumference), and that it owes its origin to such
a center. In our present state — part of our being weighed down
by body, as one might have the feet under water with all the rest
untouched — we bear ourselves aloft by that intact part, and, in

that, hold through our own center to the center of all centers, just as the centers of the great circles of a sphere coincide with that of the sphere to which all belong. Thus we rest.

Material mass cannot blend with other material mass; but unbodied things are not under this limitation; their separation is not by space but by difference of quality; in the absence of otherness, it is similars mutually present. Thus the Supreme as containing no otherness is ever present with us; we with It, when we put otherness away. The Supreme has no desire towards us, that It should center about us; but towards It we have desire, so that we center about It; but we do not always look. Thus a choir while singing might turn its attention away from the leader in the center; let it but face aright and it sings with beauty, present effectively.

We are ever before the Supreme — cut off is utter dissolution; we can no longer be — but we do not always attend; when we do look, our Term is attained; this is rest; this is the end of singing ill; effectively before their leader, the singers lift a choral song that is full of God.

In this choiring the soul looks upon the wellspring of Life and Intellect, the source of Being, fount of Good, root of Soul. We have not been cut away; we are not separate, what though the body-nature has closed about us to press us to itself; we breathe and hold our ground because the Supreme does not give and pass but gives on forever. Our being is the fuller for our turning Thither; this is our prosperity; to hold aloof is loneliness and lessening. Here is the soul's peace, outside of evil, refuge taken in the place clean of wrong; here it has true knowing; here it is immune. Here is the true living; our present life apart from God is but a mimicry.

Life in the Supreme is the native Act of Intellect; in virtue of that converse it brings forth gods, brings forth beauty, brings forth righteousness and all moral good; for of all these the soul is pregnant when it has been filled with God. This state is its first and final, because from God it comes, its good lies There, and once turned to God, it is again what it was. Life here, with the things of earth, is a sinking, a defeat, a failing of the wing. That our good is There is shown by the very love inborn with the soul; the soul, other than God, but sprung from Him, must needs love Him. So long as it is There, it holds the heavenly love; There the soul is Aphrodite of the heavens; here, turned harlot, Aphrodite of the public ways.

The soul by nature loves God and longs to be at one with Him in the noble love of a daughter for a noble father; but coming to human birth and lured by the courtships of this sphere, she takes up with another love, a mortal, leaves her father and falls. But one day coming to hate her shame, she puts off evil, once more seeks her father and finds peace.

Those to whom this experience is strange may understand by way of our earthly longings and the joy we have in winning to what we most desire, remembering always that here what we love is perishable, that our loving is of phantoms and turns awry because our Good was not here; There only is our veritable love and There we may possess It submerged no longer in the alien flesh.

He who has *seen* knows what I say, — that the soul takes on another life as it approaches God; thus restored, it feels that the Dispenser of true Life is There and that we must put aside all else and rest in This alone, This become, This alone, all the earthly environment done away, in haste to be free, impatient of any bond holding us to the baser, so that with our entire being we may cling about This, no part in us remaining but through it we may touch God.

Thus we have all the vision that may be of Him and of ourselves; but it is of a self wrought to splendor, brimmed with the Intellectual light, *become* that very light, pure, buoyant, unburdened, raised to Godhood, rather identical with God, all aflame then, but flickering out if it should take up again the discarded burden.

But how comes the soul not to keep that ground?

Because it has not yet escaped wholly; but there will be the time of vision unbroken, the self no longer vexed by any hindrance of the body. Not that those hindrances beset that in us which has veritably seen; it is the other phase of the soul that suffers and that only when we withdraw from vision and take to knowing by proof, by the processes of reason. It is not our reason that has seen; it is reason's Prior, as far above reason as the very object of that vision must be.

Our self-seeing There is a communion with the self restored to its purity. No doubt we should not speak of *seeing*, but instead of *seen* and *seer* speak boldly of a simple unity. For in this seeing we neither see nor distinguish nor are there two. The man is changed, no longer himself nor self-belonging; he is merged with the Supreme, sunken into It, one with It; only in separation is there duality. This is why the vision baffles telling; for how could a man bring back tidings of the Supreme as detached when he has seen It as one with himself? It is not to be told, not to be revealed to any that has not himself had the happiness to see. Since beholder was one with beheld, and it was not a vision compassed but a unity apprehended, the man formed by this mingling with the Supreme would, if he but remembered, carry Its image impressed upon him; he is become the Unity, having no diversity either in relation to himself or anything else; no movement now, no passion, no outlooking desire, once this ascent is achieved; reason is in abeyance and intellection and even the very self; caught away, God-possessed, in perfect stillness, all the being calmed, he turns neither to this side nor to that, nor even inwards to himself; utterly resting, he has become rest itself. He has risen beyond Beauty, the choir of the virtues overpassed; like one who, having penetrated the inner sanctuary, leaves the temple images behind; for There his converse is not with image, not with trace, but with the Deity Himself, in view of whom all the rest is but of secondary concern. This is the only seeing reserved for the sanctuary; look otherwise and there is nothing there.

Things here are but signs that show to the wise how the Supreme God is known; the enlightened priest reading the sign may enter the holy place and make the vision real. This Term, attained only by those that have overpassed all, is the All-Transcending. There is thus a converse in virtue of which the essential man outgrows Being, becomes identical with the Transcendent of Being. He that knows himself to be one with This, has in himself the likeness of the Supreme; if from that heightened self he can pass higher still — image to archetype — he has won the term of all his journeying.

This is the life of gods and of godlike and blessed men, — liberation from the alien that besets us here, a life taking no pleasure in the things of earth — a flight of the alone to the Alone.

(*Pp. 214–22*)

Lᴛᴛᴜᴛᴜᴛᴜᴛᴜᴛᴜᴛᴜᴛᴜᴛᴜᴛᴜᴛᴜᴛᴜᴛᴜᴛᴜᴛᴜᴛᴜᴛᴜᴛ

Bibliography

A BRIEF BIBLIOGRAPHY OF CLASSICAL PHILOSOPHERS

You learn to read philosophy as you learn to swim: by plunging in and trying it for yourself. But it helps no end to have someone at your side who you know can swim well enough for both of you if necessary. A good introduction to philosophy and a history of philosophy are indispensable aids to one who wants to gain the greatest value from these books of selections from the writings of philosophers. Ideas must be seen in the perspective of men, movements and philosophic traditions in order to be appreciated. The books *about* philosophy that I am suggesting are of tested merit. Undoubtedly there are many others of equal worth, though these stand among the best.

INTRODUCTIONS AND HISTORIES

DRAKE, DURANT. *Invitation to Philosophy.* New York: Houghton Mifflin Co., 1933.

PATRICK, G. T. W. *Introduction to Philosophy.* 2d ed. New York: Houghton Mifflin Co., 1935.

DURANT, WILL. *The Story of Philosophy.* New York: Simon & Schuster, 1920.

FERM, VERGILIUS. *First Adventures in Philosophy.* New York: Charles Scribner's Sons, 1936.

THILLY, FRANK. *History of Philosophy.* New York: Henry Holt & Co., 1914.

BOAS, GEORGE. *The Major Traditions of European Philosophy.* New York: Harper & Brothers, 1929.

RANDALL, J. H., JR. *The Making of the Modern Mind.* New York: Houghton Mifflin Co., 1926.

RUNES, D. D., ed. *Dictionary of Philosophy.* New York: Alliance Book Corp., 1942.

BIOGRAPHICAL BOOKS

Articles on individual philosophers in *Encyclopedia Britannica*.

TAYLOR, A. E. *Plato: The Man and His Works*. New York: Dial Press, 1936.

———. *Aristotle*. London: Oxford University Press, 1919.

ROSS, W. D. *Aristotle*. London: Oxford University Press, 1923.

INGE, W. R. *The Philosophy of Plotinus*. London: Oxford University Press, 1928.

SELECTIONS

BAKEWELL, CHARLES M. *Source Book in Ancient Philosophy*. Rev. ed. New York: Charles Scribner's Sons, 1939.

SMITH, T. V., ed. *Philosophers Speak for Themselves*. Chicago: University of Chicago Press, 1934.

EDMAN, IRWIN, ed. *The Works of Plato*. New York: Simon & Schuster, 1937.

McKEON, RICHARD, ed. *Selections from Medieval Philosophers*. 2 vols. New York: Charles Scribner's Sons, 1929.

ROBINSON, DANIEL S., ed. *An Anthology of Modern Philosophy*. New York: Thomas Y. Crowell, 1931.

MAJOR WORKS OF CLASSICAL PHILOSOPHERS

Many excellent commentaries on these philosophical works are available and are listed in detail in the books mentioned here, as well as in the various articles in the *Encyclopedia Britannica* which deal with the philosophers and their work.

PLATO. *The Dialogues of Plato,* translated by Benjamin Jowett, M.A. Edited by Richard McKeon. 2 vols. New York: Random House, 1937.

ARISTOTLE. *The Basic Works of Aristotle*. Edited by Richard McKeon. New York: Random House, 1941.

STOICS AND EPICUREANS. *The Stoic and Epicurean Philosophers*. Edited by W. J. Oates. New York: Random House, 1940.

PLOTINUS. *The Philosophy of Plotinus*. By W. R. Inge. London: Oxford University Press, 1928.

PLOTINUS. *The Enneads of Plotinus,* translated by Stephen Mc-Kenna. 5 vols. London: Medici Society, Ltd., 1917–30.

SUPPLEMENTARY READINGS

PEGIS, ANTON C. *St. Thomas and the Greeks.* Milwaukee: Marquette University Press, 1943.

SALMSEN, FRIEDRICH. *Plato's Theology.* Ithaca, N. Y.: Cornell University Press, 1942.

MORE, PAUL ELMER. *The Religion of Plato.* Princeton, N. J.: Princeton University Press, 1921.

Index